GEORGE S.
PATTON

★ ★ ★ ON GUTS, GLORY, AND WINNING ★ ★ ★

GEORGE S. PATTON

★ ★ ★ ★ ★ ★ ★ ★ ★ ★ ★ ★ ★ ★ ★ ★ ★ ★ ★

GARY BLOOMFIELD

Guilford, Connecticut

An imprint of Globe Pequot

Distributed by NATIONAL BOOK NETWORK

Copyright © 2017 by Gary Bloomfield

British Library Cataloguing in Publication Information available
Library of Congress Cataloging-in-Publication Data available

ISBN 978-1-4930-2948-8 (hardcover)
ISBN 978-1-4930-2949-5 (e-book)

∞™ The paper used in this publication meets the minimum requirements of American National Standard for Information Sciences—Permanence of Paper for Printed Library Materials, ANSI/NISO Z39.48-1992.

Printed in the United States of America

Dedicated to:

My father, Army Command Sergeant Major
Robert D. Bloomfield,
who taught me to never give in, never give up,
never back down, never back off,
and absolutely . . . never, ever quit.

His hero was George Patton.

✶✶✶✶✶✶✶✶✶✶ CONTENTS ✶✶✶✶✶✶✶✶✶✶✶✶

ACKNOWLEDGMENTS

When I was seven, my father took me to West Point, while on our way to visit relatives in Toronto. We walked the grounds, and eventually came upon the statue of General George Patton. From my viewpoint, he looked gigantic, and, after hearing my father talking about Patton's exploits during World War II, he seemed invincible. Many years later, when I was managing editor for *VFW* magazine, I relied on the public affairs office and the historians at West Point to provide reference materials, maps, and photos on a variety of military topics. I also asked for their help while researching an earlier book I did on General Patton. That research was also used to complete this book, and will be used for two more books I have planned on Patton.

I served for ten years as an Army photo-journalist, then another fourteen as an Army public affairs civilian. At each duty assignment, I was able to do research on topics I was interested in, including General Patton. At Fort Leavenworth, the back issues of *Military Review* and the historian at the post museum were invaluable, for documents, speeches, letters, and articles written by Patton. At Fort Riley, in the 1970s, I was interested in Patton, but had no intention of writing about him. Fortunately, I kept everything, so when it came time to work on this book, I simply had to find the files and dust everything off.

I spent many hours in the research library of the General George Patton Museum of Leadership at Fort Knox over several years. They graciously showed me photos, letters, paintings, and accoutrements rarely seen by the public.

At the Library of Congress and National Archives in Washington, DC, I spent long hours researching photos, not just of Patton, but World War II. Many of those photos have been used in this book.

I would also like to acknowledge the Public Affairs Office and the Command Historian for US Army Europe in Heidelberg, Germany. This was another duty assignment, and I took advantage of my off duty time, including visiting the location where Patton was involved in an automobile accident that left him paralyzed, and the military hospital where he passed away days later.

I also have to say thanks to my agent, Peter Beren, who pitched this project to Lyons Press; and my editor, Eugene Brissie, who remembered my work on two earlier books, on World War II athletes and World War II entertainers. Coincidentally, I had written about his uncle—Lou Brissie—who played baseball and was wounded in the war. And a special thanks to the design team at Lyons Press. Their efforts on my World War II athletes book earned it the Ben Franklin Award, and they've done another commendable job with this book.

Thanks muchly to everyone.

GEORGE PATTON ON HIS WRITINGS

My poetry, my rhymes,
were written by a man who,
having seen something of war
is more impressed with the manly virtues it engenders
than with the necessary and much exaggerated horrors
attendant upon it.

They are offered to the public
in the hope that they may help to counteract
the melancholy viewpoint of many of our poets
who write of the great wars.

We should not dwell on sorrow
that these slain in battle have died,
but rather be thankful that they have lived.

INTRODUCTION

George Patton had a fascination with the intricacies of war and the invincible heroes who waged it. As a boy he listened with wonderment to the tales of conquerors and warriors and envisioned fighting alongside Frederick the Great, Caesar, Hannibal, and Genghis Khan, and being a vaunted member of King Arthur's Knights of the Round Table. He imagined the glory of victory, of returning home to enduring throngs and accepting the accolades of the appreciative masses. But he also knew that sometimes the most valiant of warriors may fall in battle, and he imagined his lifeless body being carried home on his shield, battered and bloodied, or in a flag-draped coffin, buried with full military honors. (During World War II he yearned for the Medal of Honor, but he wanted it awarded posthumously.) Even as a boy, he knew one day he would be one of those conquerors who ordered men into battle, who basked in victories on distant battlefields but who also tasted the bitterness of defeats.

As a teenager and later as a military cadet, he roamed the battlegrounds of the Civil War and could see how each conflict unfolded. He heard the distant cannon fire, smelled the gunpowder, and listened to the bullets whizzing by, swords and bayonets clashing, the combatants charging forward, many of them to their death. He loved it all and was fully aware of the strategies employed by Grant and Lee, Sherman and McClellan, wondering how he would have dispatched his own troops if he had been the puppet master back then. Could he have led the

★ ★ ★

As a youngster, and later as a cadet, George Patton studied Civil War campaigns, then walked the battlefields after each battle during World War I and envisioned leading his own troops. It was a habit he continued during World War II.

Confederates to victory if only he had lived a few decades earlier? Yes, he was certain of it.

Later in World War I, he stood on French hillsides and could see the massed Roman Legions from centuries past advancing out of the mist; he saw Charlemagne and Napoleon, larger than life, conquering all who dared to oppose them.

He studied the tactics of Attila the Hun, the Valkyrie, Lord Cardigan and the Charge of the Light Brigade, and the Chinese strategist Sun Tzu. As an accomplished equestrian, he mourned the demise of the Polish Mounted Cavalry with their majestic steeds, crushed in September of 1939, when the Nazi war machine and its new battle tactic known as a Lightning War, or *Blitzkrieg*, devastated Poland. He analyzed the terrain of European battlefields, and weather patterns that would bedevil anyone attacking through the Fulda Gap or approaching the Russian Steppes, especially during those brutal winters, as both Napoleon and Hitler would cursedly regret.

During World War II, Patton studied his opponents and the playing fields they would wage war on, from North Africa to Sicily, later again in France and on into the German Fatherland. He knew almost by heart the battles that had previously been fought there. But of course he knew. Many times he would say to confidants: "I was here." Maybe it was his vivid imagination and photographic recall of the many books and maps he'd studied, but in fact, George Patton truly believed in reincarnation and that in previous lives, he had fought on those same killing fields: often victorious, sometimes defeated, but with certainty he had been there before.

His fellow officers sometimes felt he was a little bonkers, especially concerning his beliefs about reincarnation, but he chocked that up to envy.

In 1927, when Patton was a captain, Maj. Gen. W. R. Smith wrote in his efficiency report, "This man would be invaluable in time of war, but is a disturbing element in time of peace."

And decades later, Army colonel J. J. Farley was overheard saying "Patton was an acolyte to Mars."

Only God knew the fate of every warrior in combat, but George Patton certainly intended to swing the advantage in his favor as often as possible. He studied his opponents, most notably Erwin Rommel of the German Afrika Korps, assessing strengths and weaknesses, probing for tendencies, vulnerabilities. He wanted to know as much as possible of the German mindset and read the World War I memoirs of Rommel, Hans von Seeckt, and Adolf von Schell. And he patterned his own leadership style after the German concept of *Auftragstaktic*, where the commander issues an order, then allows his subordinate commanders the latitude to direct their own unit's actions in accomplishing that mission.

He wanted to know the weather conditions of battles from centuries gone, studied terrain maps to determine natural

General Patton was a voracious reader of warcraft, especially anything pertaining to previous battles waged on the same terrain as upcoming battles.

He also wanted to be near the front, to watch battles unfolding, able to redirect his forces in real time. He had no use for many of his counterparts—those armchair generals—who waged war from a safe distance, like chess masters moving pieces across a massive chess board.

obstacles, death traps, vantage points, etc. These things would never change, despite any technological advancements in weaponry. Then he would plan upcoming battles accordingly, even meticulously accounting for contingencies when things didn't go as expected. (His critics and opponents were quick to declare Patton made battle decisions without forethought, but in fact, he anticipated the enemy tactics and could counterpunch immediately before they could gain the initiative, almost as if he had a spy in their midst.)

Patton was also at the forefront of tactical innovation. During World War I he was the only American officer who recognized the future importance of slow-moving armored behemoths rumbling across the French countryside, and he volunteered to oversee the development of America's tank corps. Despite criticism from his infantry, cavalry, and artillery rivals, Patton knew someday the tank would play a decisive role on the battlefield. One thing he knew for certain—trench warfare was no way to seize the advantage and put a quick end to the enemy.

After World War I, when Patton was stationed in Hawaii, he made the brash declaration that someday the Japanese would attack Pearl Harbor. Of course no one took him seriously because he was just a junior Army officer, who knew nothing about naval tactics.

In addition to writing numerous papers (including predicting the Pearl Harbor attack), Patton was also a prolific poet, and wrote the following in 1922, a few years after the Great War, and a decade before world events in Europe and the Far East would escalate into another world war:

THROUGH A GLASS, DARKLY

Through the travail of the ages,
midst the pomp and toil of war,
Have I fought and strove and perished
countless times upon this star.
In the forms of many people,
in all panoplies of time
Have I seen the luring vision
of the Victory Maid, sublime.

I have battled for fresh mammoth,
I have warred for pastures new,
I have listened to the whispers
when the race track instinct grew.
I have known the call to battle,
in each changeless changing shape
From the high souled voice of conscience
to the beastly lust for rape.

I have sinned and I have suffered,
played the hero and the knave;
Fought for belly, shame, or country
and for each have found a grave
I cannot name my battles,
for the visions are not clear,
Yet, I see the twisted faces
and I feel the rending spear.

Perhaps I stabbed our Savior
in His sacred helpless side.
Yet, I've called His name in blessing
when in after times I died.
In the dimness of the shadows,
where we hairy heathens warred,
I can taste in thought the lifeblood;
we used teeth before the sword.

While in later clearer vision
I can sense the coppery sweat,
Feel the pikes grow wet and slippery,
when our Phalanx, Cyrus met.
Hear the rattle of the harness,
where the Persian darts bounced clear,
See their chariots wheel in panic,
from the Hoplites' leveled spear.

See the mole grow monthly longer,
reaching for the walls of Tyre.
Hear the crash of tons of granite,
smell the quenchless eastern fire.
Still more clearly as a Roman,
can I see the Legion close,
As our third rank moved in forward
and the short sword found our foes.

Once again I feel the anguish
of that blistering treeless plain
When the Parthian showered death bolts,
and our discipline was vain.
I remember all the suffering
of those arrows in my neck.
Yet, I stabbed a grinning savage
as I died upon my back.

Once again I smell the heat sparks,
when my Flemish plate gave way
and the lance ripped through my entrails
as on Crecy's field I lay
In the windless, blinding stillness
of the glittering tropic sea
I can see the bubbles rising
where we set the captives free.

Midst the spume of half a tempest,
I have heard the bulwarks go
When the crashing, point blank round
shot sent destruction to our foe.
I have fought with gun and cutlass
on the red and slippery deck
With all Hell aflame within me
and a rope around my neck.

And still later as a General
have I galloped with Murat
While we laughed at death and numbers,
trusting in the Emperor's Star.
Till at last our star had faded,
and we shouted to our doom
Where the sunken road of Ohain
closed us in its quivering gloom.

So but now with Tanks a'clatter
have I waddled on the foe
Belching death at twenty paces,
by the star shell's ghastly glow.
So as through a glass, and darkly
the age long strife I see
Where I fought in many guises,
many names—but always me.

And I see not in my blindness
what the objects were I wrought,
But as God rules o'er our bickering,
it was through His will I fought.
So forever in the future,
shall I battle as of yore,
Dying to be born a fighter,
but to die again, once more.

Death found in him no faltering,
but faithful to the last
He smiled into the face of Fate
and mocked it as he passed.
No, death to him was not defeat,
but victory sublime
The grave promoted him
to be a hero for all time.

In the 1930s, when Nazi Germany sent a combined force, known as the Condor Legion, to Spain, Patton heard about a devastatingly efficient new way of conducting war. Known as blitzkrieg, it combined the rapidly advancing forces of infantry, armor, and aviation, augmented by long-range artillery to overwhelm the enemy. The Spanish Civil War was merely a prelude to what the Nazis unveiled to the world when they rumbled across Poland in September of 1939, opposed by little more than mounted cavalry.

Patton developed his own version of rapid advance and by the end of World War II, he was employing blitzkrieg tactics even better than the Nazis. In fact he was the only Allied commander the Nazi High Command respected. German Army General Gunther Blumentritt stated, "We regarded General Patton extremely highly as the most aggressive panzer-general of the Allies. His operations impressed us enormously, probably because he came closest to our own concept of the classical military commander. He even improved on Napoleon's basic tenet— *activité, vitesse—vitesse*" ["Activite, Activite, Vitesse!"].

And Heinz Guderian, the Wehrmacht's tactical genius stated, "I hear much about General Patton and he conducted a good campaign. From the standpoint of a tank specialist, I must congratulate him on his victory since he acted as I would have done had I been in his place."

Yet despite the advances in weaponry, Patton knew that ultimately wars are fought by those young warriors on the frontlines. From studying the past, he knew armies that weren't trained and

★ ★ ★

Wars begin when diplomacy fails, and then it becomes a conflict of man against man. The weaponry becomes more lethal from one decade to the next, but it is still man inflicting his will on his enemies while loved ones at home wait, hopeful but helpless.

conditioned for battle could be easily defeated, so he drilled his forces to the point of exhaustion, without regard for how they felt about it or what they thought of him. He trained his armies to be disciplined yet ruthless on the battlefield, superior to any opponent they might face. He wanted his soldiers to develop what he called a "warrior's soul." He believed in it and expected every single soldier in his command to have it. He had little tolerance for anyone who showed weakness.

During World War II there were many great units that distinguished themselves in battle, and those soldiers certainly have a right to be proud that they fought at Normandy, or Sicily, during Operation Torch or the Battle of the Bulge, or wherever it is they fought and defeated Hitler and his Thousand Year Reich. Those who are most proud will simply say "I served with Patton," knowing nothing more needs to be said.

Here then, in all its brutal honesty and wicked humor is a glimpse into the psyche and the soul of America's ultimate war fighter . . . the incomparable George S. Patton, World War II warrior, par excellence.

THE EARLY WAR YEARS POEMS

The horrors and ugliness of war are in stark contrast to the lyricism of poetry. George Patton was an avid reader of poetry, including the battle poems of Walt Whitman, Robert Frost, Nathaniel Hawthorne, and Ambrose Bierce. He was also a voracious reader of both fictitious tales and historic retellings of famous battles and commanders. He was a prolific poet, though much of his verse is crude, shocking, sometimes hilarious, and does not measure up to those more skilled in the craft.

The common misperception of George Patton is of a brash, impulsive (and erratic) commander, willing to sacrifice his troops without conscience. In fact, he cared deeply about the combatants he led into battle. He may not have revealed his feelings to anyone but his closest confidants, but he does confess his pride, his guilt, and his regrets in his many poems.

During the early 1900s, leading up to World War I, he often wrote rhyming verse, with occasional forays into free verse. With his battle experiences in the Great War, Patton could inject his writings with the sights and smells, the victories, and the tragedies that only a combat veteran knows firsthand.

WAR (1909)

Oh! thou uncrowned mistress of all time
Since first man thought his brother man to slay
Be not disgusted with our sudden state
Nor fail in future with thy sons to stay.

What though cursed striving over useless dross
Has ruined half the soul God gave to man
And made him as the swinish beasts that strive
To swill their bellies with what e'er they can.

What though the genius made for nobler things
He planned with coward zeal to scale the sky
And gliding up unseen to dastard hurl
Death and destruction on all standing nigh.

Fear not great Mistress of the great in man
There still exists and must until the end
A strength which dastard cunning cannot quench
Which avarice cannot as dollars spend.

For which man lives and moves upon the sphere
His path shall now as e'er be marked by war
And he who on that path would leave a step
Must guide him in accordance with thy law.

For when the rich, the brilliant, and the great
Shall stand in nakedness before their God
How shall the glory of the gold or pin
Compare with that which from thy sword has flowed?

We look upon the lengthened scroll of time
And Croesus is eclipsed by Bonaparte
What name of Milton, Dante or Shakespeare
May dare to stand with Caesar in the heart?

Then grieve not Goddess of the nobly great
Though sad faced Peace overshadoweth the earth
Tis but the darkness of the coming day
And soon of war thy sons shall have no dearth.

And on every hand though hearest as now
Men prate of Peace and all that it has done
Smile and remember were it not for Thee
Man still would slay his quarry with a stone.

For had not in the early dawn of life
Man warred with ape which ranked then with him
We still should swing in jungles by our tails
And chattering, leap with cries from limb to limb.

Had not the Christian stood against the Turk
And struggled glorious in bloody war
We now perchance should be debased as they
Looking with lust in all of good we saw.

Why then, oh Goddess, since times are as e'er
Should war be now so decadent and cursed?
Why should its good which oft has saved the world
Be now so much confounded with its worst?

Is it not possible that soon again
A worse than Turk shall raise his hand to slay?
And naught that all of glassy peace may do
Shall stop his hand until thou bidst him stay.

For though at times the world has been accursed
By greed of land, of gold, of worldly gain
Never has been such danger as may come
From senseless envy sown in common brain.

So true it is that in all walks of peace
Genius stands out but in one form exposed
While with the worshippers who follow war
Genius must stand in all her state disclosed.

ETERNAL PEACE (1916)

Since the ancient Christian zealots
With an early Christian smile
Beat out the brains of heathens
In a very righteous style

Down the passion-clouded ages
To the Inquisition's time
Have all sorts of other bigots
Practice every sort of crime.

The Round Heads with intolerance
Lopped the curly heads off peers
Singing psalms the while they rotted
Stuck aloft on grisly spears.

And the pious folk of Salem
Burned their witches with great glee
Fully confident that Heaven
Took delight such sights to see.

So today in equal folly
Do our Pacifists assail
Those who still upholding honor
The Millennium will not hail.

Yes, these last demented creatures
Seek with words to crucify
Those, who for their country's honor,
Still are not afraid to die.

Yet as surely as these others
Have at last been held to shame
So will future generations
Our poor Pacifists defame.

For a thousand years ahead of us
Will you as surely find
The world as full of passion
As a thousand years behind.

For mankind is just as warlike
As it was before the flood
And the clay which molds us moderns
Is the same old blood-soaked mud.

BILL (1918)

Bill, he kept racin' the motor,
for fear that the damned thing would die.
While I fiddled 'round with the breech block
and wished for a piece of your pie.

It's funny the way it affects you,
When you're waitin' for the signal to go.
There's none of the high moral feeling
About which the newspapers blow.

For myself, I always is hungry,
While Bill thought his spark plugs was foul.
Some guys talks o' sprees they has been on,
and one kid, what's croaked, thought of school.

At last, I seen Number One signal;
I beat on the back o' Bill's neck.
He slipped her the juice and she started,
and Bill he ain't never come back.

The first news we had of the Boches
Was shot splinters, right in the eye.
I cussed twice as loud as the Colonel,
and forgot all about the old pie.

A Boche he runs out with a tank gun;
I gave him H.E. in the guts.
You ought to have seen him pop open!
They sure was well fed, was them sluts.

We wiped out two nests with case shot,
and was just gettin' into a third,
When we plunked in a hole full of water.
That God-damned Bill sure was a bird.

He hollers, "Frank, you're married;
If only one gets out, it's you."
and he rammed me up out of the turret . . .
I guess that's about all I knew.

A stinkin' whizz–bang beaned me,
Or I might of rescued Bill,
But it's too late now. He's sleepin'
By our tank, on that God-damned hill.

They gave him a Medal of Honor,
For savin' me for you,
So if it's a boy we'll name it Bill,
It's the least and the most we can do.

★ ★ ★

George Patton not only led men into battle, but he also helped develop the advances in weaponry between the end of the Great War and World War II. His poems reveal the psyche of the man, a complex Spartan warrior.

This poem, based on his experiences in World War I with trench warfare and poison gas, personifies the moon as a woman looking down on the battlefield still littered with the dead and wounded.

MOON AND THE DEAD (1918)

The road of the battle languished,
*   The hate from the guns was still,*
*   While the moon rose up*
*   from a smoke cloud,*
*   and looked at the dead on the hill.*

Pale was her face with anguish,
*   Wet were her eyes with tears,*
*   As she gazed on the twisted corpses,*
*   Cut off in their earliest years.*

Some were bit by the bullet,
  Some were kissed by the steel,
    Some were crushed by the cannon,
      But all were still, how still!

The smoke wreaths hung in the hollows,
  The blood stink rose in the air;
    and the moon looked down in pity,
      At the poor dead lying there.

Light of their childhood's wonder,
  Moon of their puppy love,
    Goal of their first ambition,
      She watched them from above.

Yet not with regret she mourned them,
  Fair slain on the field of strife,
    Fools only lament the hero,
      Who gives for faith his life.

She sighed for the lives extinguished,
  She wept for the loves that grieve,
    But she glowed with pride on seeing,
      That manhood still doth live.

The moon sailed on contented,
  Above the heaps of slain,
    For she saw that manhood liveth,
      and honor breathes again.

L'ENVOI (1916)

When the last great battle is finished
and the last great general shall fall,
When the roar of the mighty guns is dumb
as the kiss of the nickeled ball.

When the screams of the dying that mixed
With the shout that the living give out
As they rush on the foe,
When the mixed noise of an army in flight
The gasp and the curse and the shouting are low,

When soldiers have ceased to struggle,
When war is raged with the tongue,
When men are praised for cowardice
And men for bravery hung,

When honor and virtue and courage
Are fled like departing day
As the cursed shape of eternal peace
Comes up on the evening gray,

When money is God and Lord of all
and liars alone have weight,
When the road to heaven is barred with gold
and wide yawns Hell's black gate —

★ ★ ★

George Patton, studying many of the great commanders in history, felt a leader should be at the front with his unit, exposed to the same dangers as his troops. While leading his tank battalion up a hill near Cheppy in World War I, he faced enemy machine gun fire, pinned down by the fusillade. "I felt a great desire to run, I was trembling with fear when suddenly I thought of my progenitors and seemed to see them in a cloud over the German lines looking at me. I became calm at once and saying aloud, 'It is time for another Patton to die,' called for volunteers and went forward to what I honestly believed to be certain death," Patton later wrote. Still under fire and wounded in the skirmish, he remained to coordinate the Allied attack until he was evacuated and patched up. There were many more instances in the Great War and during World War II when Patton was exposed to danger and refused to pull back out of harm's way.

Then those who live in servile chains
To filthy lucre slaves
Ah, how they will yearn for the soldier's life
and for the hero's grave, and will say as they sadly think of it:
War was a priceless benefit, although a sacrifice.

THE END OF WAR (1917)

When the hairy apes of long ago
*   Battled for days to see*
Whether the tails of future apes
*   Should straight or curly be.*

Other apes whose hair more sparsely grew
*   And the shes who were great with child*
Hung from branches up side down
*   And sighed, and gibbered, and smiled.*

They said: "Such sights are hardly nice
*   "For tails are what they are.*
"'Tis savage and like the wolves,
*   "This must be the end of war."*

When the painted savages of the swamps
*   Slew the clay-daubed men of the brae*
In order to settle by flint and club
*   Which clan might draw mammoths on clay,*

The craven lake-folk, smeared with fat,
　　Crouched on their rafts and said;
"Though insects bite us through our grease
　　"Tis better than being dead."

"Our cultured smell makes us despised
　　"We live a mildewed life
"But we are the people of brotherly love.
　　"This MUST be the end of strife."

The gentle Persian fled before
　　The warlike men of Greece;
The phalanx broke their masses
　　So they advocated peace.

They praised the purple coated fop
　　Whose hands were white and slim;
They loathed the sweaty brute in bronze
　　And, loathing, fled from him.

While huddled in their harlots' arms
　　Their land in flames they saw;
Yet kissed the painted odalisques
　　And cried: "Tis the end of war."

When Carthage conquered far off Spain
　　And all but conquered Rome
She suffered from the lethargy
　　Of fighting far from home.

She deified domestic quiet
  Her youth would no more fight
Till bloody Zama's fatal day
  Destroyed for e'er her might.

For having conquered Spain she thought
  Like countless fools before
That having gained her peace by strife
  There would be no more war.

'Twere idle further to recount
  The folly of mankind
Who gaining all by battle
  To future wars grows blind.

The folly of the slogan
  Down all the ages rings
The ruins of republics
  The funeral dirge of kings.

"At last the strife is ended;
  "Battles shall rage no more;
"The time of perfect peace has come;
  "There CAN be no more war."

Still, like the foolish revelers
  In Babylon's banquet hall
They'll take their ease while mocking
  The writing on the wall.

They will disband their armies
  When this great strife is won,
And trust again to pacifists
  To guard for them their home.

They will return to futileness
  As quickly as before
Though Truth and History vainly shout
  "THERE IS NO END TO WAR."

CHAPTER 2

STUDYING
THE MYSTERIES OF WAR

Growing up, George Patton loved to read tales of knights in shining armor slaying fiery dragons and rescuing damsels in distress; of Nordic warriors venturing far beyond the known worlds to conquer any and all who dared to resist them. He knew he would someday lead great armies into battle, and studied both the written works of the great commanders of historic conquests, and the current strategists, even those with sound yet unproven theories of war.

As a young cadet, he was especially interested in Prussian Marshal Helmuth von Moltke, who felt civilizations could thrive after the turmoil of warfare. Patton also wanted to know as much as possible about his opponents and even the peoples who lived in the regions where he was about to wage war.

Before the Allied invasion of North Africa, he wanted to know more about the Arab way of thinking, and so he studied the Koran. To say he was a student of war, long into his later years, would be an understatement. Patton never stopped learning and improving what he knew best . . . warcraft.

One continues to learn about war by practicing war.

Patton was an early proponent of tanks, leading back to the Great War when armor tactics were still in their infancy. In 1917 he led the United States Tank Corps when it first tasted victory, at Cambrai in France. A year later he was at the front near the Meuse-Argonne offensive, directing his armor units when he was wounded in the leg.

Despite great peril in World War II, Patton would continue to lead and direct his troops at the front. In mid-1944, he wrote about an amusing sight that reminded him of World War I: "We drove on to Bourg, my tank brigade headquarters in 1918. The first man I saw in the street was standing on the same manure pile whereon I am sure he had perched in 1918. I asked if he had been there during the last war, to which he replied, 'Oh yes, General Patton, and you were here then as a colonel.'"

I have been studying the subject of war for forty odd years. When a surgeon decides in the course of an operation to change its objective, to splice that artery or cut deeper and remove another which he finds infected, he is not making a snap judgement, but one based on knowledge, experience, and training. SO AM I!

Despite the oceans of ink and years of thought which have been devoted to the elucidation of war, its secrets still remain shrouded in mystery. Indeed, it is due largely to the very volume of available information that the veil is so thick. War is an art and as such it is not susceptible to explanation by fixed formulae. Yet, from the earliest time there has been an unending effort to subject its complex and emotional structure to dissection, to enunciate rules for its waging, to make tangible its intangibility. One might as well attempt to isolate the soul by the dissection of a cadaver as to seek the essence of war by the analysis of its records.

Volumes are devoted to armament; pages to inspiration.

I believe that for a man to become a great soldier it is necessary for him to be so thoroughly conversant with all sorts of military possibilities that whenever an occasion arises, he has at hand, without effort on his part, a parallel. To attain this end, I believe that it is necessary for a man to begin to read military history in its earliest and crudest form and to follow it down in natural sequence, permitting his mind to grow with his subject until he can grasp, without any effort, the most abstract question of the Science of War because he is already permeated with its elements.

The M1 rifle is the greatest battle implement ever devised.

Papa always told me that the first thing was to be a good soldier. Next was to be a good scholar.

Prepare for the unknown by studying how others in the past have coped with the unforeseeable and the unpredictable.

For years I have been accused of making snap judgments. Honestly, this is not the case because I am a profound military student and the thoughts I express, perhaps too flippantly, are the result of years of thought and study.

* ★ ★

It took me a long time to realize just how much a student of
medieval history could gain from observing the Arab.

—————————— ★ ★ ★ ——————————

*Infantry soldiers are known as ground-pounders because they typically have to walk, but Pat-
ton saw the stupidity in this philosophy. Not only did it wear them out before they even got to
the battle, it also delayed the action, allowing the enemy to dig in (or retreat). "When, early in
the campaign, I had issued orders that at least one regimental combat team of infantry should
ride on the tanks of an armored division, the 5th Infantry Division complained most bitterly,
stating, among other things, that there was nothing for the men to hold on to. I told them that
was the men's hard luck, but I was sure soldiers would rather ride on anything for 25 miles
than walk 15 miles," Patton would write in his journal, in mid-1944.*

We disregard the lessons of history.

Every commander wanted to believe he knew the secret to success on the battlefield. Those who were infantry officers placed their faith in the ground-pounders. Airborne officers were willing to risk it all to prove their paratroopers could descend behind the lines and create mischief. And George Patton was a tanker, America's leading proponent for armor warfare.

Army Air Corps commanders believed they could pound the hell out of the enemy, thus relegating the Army to mere mop-up duty.

During a lull in the fighting, Army soldiers watched with fascination as an aerial dogfight crisscrossed the skies over Fortress Europe, many of them wishing they could dodge bullets while dancing among the clouds instead of wallowing in the mud.

I am convinced that more emphasis should be placed on history. The purpose of history is to learn how human beings react when exposed to the danger of wounds or death, and how high ranking individuals react when submitted to the onerous responsibility of conducting war or the preparation of war.

Aviation cannot take prisoners nor hold ground.

We all feel that indiscriminate bombing has no military value and that it is cruel and wasteful and that all such efforts should always be on purely military targets and on selected commodities which are scarce for the enemy. In the case of Germany, the target would be oil.

CHAPTER 3

LORD GOD OF BATTLES

(Excerpt from a speech to the 2nd Armored Division, December of 1941)

The God of our Fathers, known of old,
  Lord of our far flung battle line.
Beneath who's awful hand we hold
  Dominion over palm and pine.

The Earth is full of anger,
  To seas are dark with wrath,
The Nations in their harness
  Go up against our path!

Ere yet we loose the legions—
  Ere yet we draw the blade.
Jehova of the thunders,
  Lord God of Battles, aid!

E'en now their vanguard gathers,
  E'en now we face the fray—
As Thou didst help our fathers,
  Help Thou our host today!
Fulfilled of signs and wonders,
  In life, in death made clear—
Jehova of the Thunders,
  Lord God of Battles, hear!

★ ★ ★

Advancing on the enemy was always a perilous task and General Patton was adamant that his units not allow terrain to dictate their avenue of approach. In fact, "it is much better to go over difficult ground where you are not expected than it is over good ground where you are. . . ."

THE SOUL IN BATTLE (1922–1924)

In the valley of the slaughter
where the winged Valkyrie dwell
And the souls of men go naked to their God
I have seen the curtain parted.
I have glimpsed the flinty trail
The final road the spirits have all trod.

Yet in the awesome clearness
of the future there made plane
The spirit loses something of its dread
And life with all its littleness is very, very drab
While the living view the corpses as not dead.

The veneer of life is melted
by the hot blast of the shell.
And we behold our fellows very plain.
Not as cur or fool or hero
but like some poor flustered thing
A trembling beast reluctant to be slane.

CHAPTER 4

CHARIOTS OF WAR

Patton survived the trench warfare and stalemate strategy of World War I; he studied Nazi Germany's blitzkrieg strategies in Spain (known as the Condor Legion), and in September of 1939, when they steamrollered Poland; and he tested his own theories of rapid advance during war maneuvers in the States. Later in North Africa, Sicily, and France he perfected his theories, and believed the key to victory was to devastate the enemy as quickly as possible, with overwhelming force.

> In a modern infantry division, if every available vehicle—tanks, armored cars, gun carriages, AA guns and trucks—is utilized, no soldier need or should walk until he actually enters battle. While the sight of a division moving under this system is abhorrent to the best instincts of a Frederickan soldier, it results in rapid advance with minimum fatigue.

There is only one tactical principle which is not subject to change. It is, "To use the means at hand to inflict the maximum amount of wounds, death and destruction on the enemy in the minimum amount of time."

I do not fear failure. I only fear the "slowing up" of the engine inside of me which is pounding, saying, "Keep going, someone must be on the top, why not YOU?"

Now that sounds like "what a great man George Patton is," but I did not have anything to do with it. The people who actually did it are the younger officers and the soldiers of the Third Army.

★ ★ ★

Patton believed in overwhelming firepower to devastate and decimate the enemy. Aerial bombardment and long-range artillery rained down hell, but it still took ground forces—infantry supported with tanks—to totally rout the German army.

His philosophy was very simple: "L'audace, l'audace, toujours l'audace." (Audacity, audacity, always audacity.) Translated, Patton expected his units to advance, no matter what the obstacles might be, advance, no excuses . . . ADVANCE.

Certainly, the advent of the atomic bomb was not half as startling as the initial appearance of gunpowder. In my own lifetime, I can remember two inventions, or possibly three, which were supposed to stop war; namely the dynamite cruiser "Vesuvius," the submarine, and the tank. Yet, wars go blithely on and will still go on when your great grandchildren are very old men.

Today, machines hold the place formally occupied by the jawbone of an ass, elephant, armor, longbow, gunpowder, and submarine. They, too, shall pass.

It is very easy for ignorant people to think that success in war may be gained by the use of some wonderful invention rather than by hard fighting and superior leadership.

The initial appearance of each new weapon or military device has always marked the zenith of its tactical effect, though usually the nadir of its technical efficiency.

THE PRECIOUS BABIES (1918)

Up and down the roadways,
through the German ranks,
Nosing out machine guns,
come the baby tanks.

Scrambling through the crater,
splashing through the pool,
Like the Usher's happy boys,
bounding out of school.

Fritz is great on wirefields,
trust the Boche for that,
But his choicest efforts
fall extremely flat.

Wasted in the weaving
of laborious days,
When the merry infant class
scampers through the maze.

Cheerful little children
of an American brain,
Winning ravished country
back to France again.

On thru town and village,
shepherded by Yanks
Romping, blithe and rollicking,
roll the baby tanks.

In the summer of 1918, a group of soldiers of the 301st Tank
Brigade, which I commanded, was having 37mm gun practice which I was observing. One defective round exploded
in the muzzle, wounding two or three men. The next round
exploded in the breech, blowing off the head of the gunner.
The men were reluctant to fire the next round, so it was
incumbent on me, as the senior officer present, to do so. In
fact, I fired three rounds without incident. This restored the
confidence of the men in the weapon. I must admit that I
have never in my life been more reluctant to pull a trigger.

The grave of that national hero, "Abandoned Rear," was still
maintained by the natives. It originated in this manner. In
1917, the mayor, who lived in the "new house" at Bourg,
bearing the date 1760, came to me, weeping copiously, to say
that we had failed to tell him of the death of one of my soldiers. Being unaware of this sad fact and not liking to admit
it to a stranger, I stalled until I found out that no one was
dead.

However, he insisted that we visit the "grave," so we went
together and found a newly closed latrine pit with the earth
properly banked and a stick at one end to which was affixed

crosswise a sign saying, "Abandoned Rear." This the French had taken for a cross. I never told them the truth.

. . . the XX Corps had captured intact . . . the whole of the Imperial Spanish Riding Academy which had left Vienna on the approach of the Russians. This Academy had been running in Vienna since the time of Charles V of Spain.

Originally the gyrations taught the horses were of military importance. That is, the courbette, or half-rear, was for the purpose of letting the horse come down at the same time that the sword was swung, so as to give the latter more force; the volte, or demi-volte, was for the purpose of avoiding attack; while the leap into the air, striking out fore and aft with the feet, was for the purpose of extricating the rider from too close contact with the enemy, and so on. With the passing years and changes in the art of war, the purpose of this form of equitation was forgotten, and the movements were taught as of value in themselves. In other words, people began, as in many other arts, to glorify the means rather than the end which the means were supposed to produce.

. . . it struck me as rather strange that, in the midst of a world at war, some twenty young and middle-aged men in great physical condition, together with about thirty grooms, had spent their entire time teaching a group of horses to wiggle their butts and raise their feet in consonance with certain signals from the heels and reins. Much as I like horses, this seemed to me wasted energy. On the other hand, it is probably wrong to permit any highly developed art, no matter how fatuous, to perish from the earth—and which arts are fatuous depends on the point of view. To me the high-schooling of horses is certainly more interesting than either painting or music.

When man first began fighting man, he unquestionably used his teeth, toenails and fingernails. Then one day a very terrified or else very inventive genius picked up a rock and bashed a man in the head while he was gnawing at his vitals. The news of this unheard of weapon unquestionably shocked Neolithic Society, but they became accustomed to

★ ★ ★

High mobility reached a new level when George Patton unleashed his version of the blitzkrieg, even startling Nazi armor commanders who had participated in the lopsided victories in Poland and the early battles in North Africa. When they got to France and northern Europe, Patton's Third Army frequently advanced more than forty miles a day. In August of 1944 alone, they penetrated more than four hundred miles toward Germany.

The advance ground to a crawl when the infantry soldiers dismounted for house-to-house fighting.

it. Thousands of years later, another genius picked up the splintered rib of a Mastodon and using it as a dagger, thrust it into the gentleman with a rock in his hand. Again, prehistoric society was shocked and said, "There will surely be no more wars. Did you hear about the Mastodon bone?"

When the shield, slingshot, javelin and the sword and armor were successively invented, each in its turn was heralded by the proponents as a means of destroying the world or of stopping war.

CHAPTER 5

FIRST TEST OF BATTLE

DUTY (1945)

Duty that armed Abraham's hand
  And nerved the blade of Antony
    Thy lambent light n'er brighter burned
      Than in this bloody war today.

It steadies in its darkest hour
  The wavering heart of womanhood
    It makes the boy to sacrifice his life,
      his all for country's good.

Oh! mighty soul, uplifting thought
  That did inspire the great of yore
    Thou hast returned into our midst
      Pray God thou ne'er shall leave us more.

Order of the Day: The Invasion of North Africa

We are now on our way to force a landing on the coast of
Northwest Africa. We are to be congratulated because we
have been chosen as the units of the United States Army to
take part in this great American effort.

Our mission is threefold. First to capture a beachhead,
second to capture the city of Casablanca, third to move

------------------------------ ★ ★ ★ ------------------------------

When the roar of Allied transport planes disrupted the skies over Casablanca, searchlights
scanned back and forth. Those planes were carrying paratroopers to be dropped behind the lines,
kicking off Operation Torch, the invasion of North Africa. Far out to sea, General Patton was
on board the warship Augusta, *waiting to follow his troops ashore.*

★ ★ ★

Operation Torch—the invasion of North Africa—was a multi-pronged attack, including transport planes, troop ships, and naval task forces, all converging on the African coast.

George Patton was on board the warship USS Augusta and as it approached North Africa, he issued orders to his troops of the Western Task Force—thirty-five thousand strong—prior to kicking off Operation Torch.

There would be several beach landings, from North Africa to Sicily, Anzio to Normandy, reminding Patton of previous conquests: "The city and harbor of Syracuse are to me of particular interest because this place probably has been the scene of more amphibious operations than any other harbor in the world. When looking over its water I could almost see the Greek triremes, the Roman galleys, the Vandals, the Arabs, the Crusaders, the French, the English, and the Americans, who, to mention only a few, have successively stormed, or attempted to storm, that harbor."

against the German wherever he may be and destroy him. We may be opposed by a limited number of Germans. It is not known whether the French Army will contest our landing. It is regrettable to contemplate the necessity of fighting the gallant French, who are at heart sympathetic, but all resistance, by whomever offered, must be destroyed.

When the great day of battle comes, remember your training and remember that speed and vigor of attack are the sure roads to success. And you must succeed, for to retreat is as cowardly as it is fatal. Americans do not surrender. During the first days and nights after you get ashore you must work unceasingly, regardless of sleep, regardless of food. A pint of sweat will save a gallon of blood.

The eyes of the world are watching us . . . God is with us . . .We will surely win.

There was a low ceiling of some 25,000 feet, with rain and wind, and all our searchlights . . . were working, probing holes in the clouds. Presently the light anti-aircraft began going off at a great rate, with tracers looking like fireflies. This continued for about five minutes and suddenly there was a tremendous flash from which came long octopus-like tentacles of fire with bulbs along them.

At intervals along the flaming shore, searchlights would suddenly flare and sweep the water. Whenever one of these searchlights flickered on, innumerable tracer bullets from our destroyers and patrol boats hurried toward it like bees returning to the hive. That searchlight immediately went out.

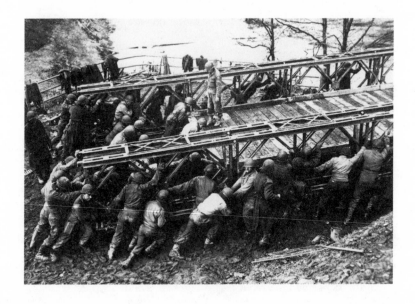

It was a long way from North Africa to northern Europe, when allied forces crossed the Rhine River and finally penetrated the German Fatherland.

CHAPTER 6

FIT TO FIGHT

George Patton didn't give a damn if his men liked him, or hated him. His only concern was to accomplish the mission, and keep as many of his boys alive as possible. And the best way to do that was to train them under battle conditions, even to the point of exhaustion, and then push them even further. He wanted them to work as a well-oiled machine, and, during massive war games in 1939 and 1940—known as the Louisiana Maneuvers—trained them under extreme conditions, preparing them for battles to come.

I believe that in war, the good of the individual must be subordinated to the good of the Army.

If we take the generally accepted definition of bravery as a quality which knows not fear, I have never seen a brave man. All men are frightened. The more intelligent they are the more they are frightened. The courageous man is the man

Never one to waste time, Patton instilled discipline in every unit he commanded, whether it was an individual tank crew or thousands of combatants. His training was demanding, his dictates inflexible, but his reasoning was clear as crystal: discipline and rapid advance in battle saves lives.

who forces himself, in spite of his fear, to carry on. Discipline, pride, self-respect, self-confidence, and the love of glory are attributes which will make a man courageous even if he is afraid.

Lack of discipline at play means the loss of the game. Lack of discipline in war means death or defeat, which is worse than death. The prize of a game is nothing. The prize of war is the greatest of all prizes . . . Freedom.

It is better to live in the limelight for a year than in the wings forever.

The purposes of discipline and training are; 1. To insure obedience and orderly movement. 2. To produce synthetic courage. 3. To provide methods of combat. 4. To prevent or delay the breakdown of the first three due to the excitement of battle.

I believe in the old and sound rule that an ounce of sweat will save a gallon of blood.

★ ★ ★

They only learned the basics of soldiering at Basic Training . . . how to march and shoot and throw a grenade. How to thrust and parry with a bayonet. How to smoke and cuss and play craps! How to take orders and do as they were told and never, ever volunteer.

At the end of it, these recruits could call themselves soldiers, but they wouldn't be accepted as combatants until they'd been stung under fire. For those untested soldiers assigned to Patton's Third Army, he expected them to learn fast because they would have to hit the ground running, and get thrown into the fight without time to learn how to stay alive. Some learned those lessons quickly, some didn't.

When at the beginning of the football season the quarter-back barks his numbers at the crouching players he excites an innate opposition; the feeling of "why in the hell should I do what he says?" Yet until that feeling is banished by habit, the team is dead on its feet. The soldier at attention and saluting is putting himself in the same frame of mind as the player; alert, on his toes, receptive. In battle, the officers are the quarterbacks, the men are the disciplined team on their toes, with that lightning response to orders which means victory and the lack of which mean death and defeat.

Since the necessary limitations of map problems inhibit the student from considering the effects of hunger, emotion, personality, fatigue, leadership and many other imponderable yet vital factors, he first neglects and then forgets them.

Discipline, which is but mutual trust and confidence, is the key to all success in peace or war.

The leader must be an actor. He is unconvincing unless he lives the part. The fixed determination to acquire the "Warrior Soul" and having acquired it, to conquer or perish with honor is the secret of victory.

Officers who fail to perform their duty by correcting small violations and in enforcing proper conduct are incapable of leading.

I don't measure a man's success by how high he climbs but by how high he bounces when he hits bottom.

If brevity is the soul of wit, then repetition is the heart of instruction.

War is just like boxing. When you get your opponent on the ropes you must keep punching the hell out of him and not let him recover.

It is the common experience of mankind that in moments of great excitement the conscious mental processes of the brain no longer operate. All actions are subconscious, the result of habits. Troops whose training and discipline depend on conscious thought become helpless crowds in battle. To send forth such men is murder. Hence, in creating an Army, we must strive at the production of soldiers, so trained that in the midst of battle they will still function.

War is not a contest with gloves. It is resorted to only when laws, which are rules, have failed.

The wrestling adage, "There is a block for every hold" is equally applicable to war. Each new weapon demands a new block and it is mightily potent until that block is devised.

The most vital quality which a soldier can possess is self confidence; utter, complete and bumptious. You can have doubts about your good looks, about your intelligence, or about your self control, but to win in war, you must have no doubt about your ability as a soldier.

Few men are killed by the bayonet, many are scared by it. Bayonets should be fixed when the fire fight starts.

The fierce frenzy of hate and determination flashing from the bloodshot eyes squinting behind the glittering steel is what wins wars.

War is conflict. Fighting is an elemental exposition of the age old effort to survive. It is the cold glitter in the attacker's eye, not the point of the questing bayonet that breaks the line.

The fear of having their guts explored with cold steel in the hands of battle-maddened men has won many a fight.

When the great day of battle comes, remember your training, and remember, above all, that speed and vigor of attack are the sure roads to success and that you must succeed. To retreat is as cowardly as it is fatal.

We are ready. I shall be delighted to lead you men against any enemy. I am confident that your disciplined valor and high training will bring victory.

If you can't get them to salute when they should salute and wear the clothes you tell them to wear, how are you going to get them to die for their country?

When you, here, every one of you, were kids, you all admired the champion marble player, the fastest runner, the toughest boxer, the big league ball players and the All-American football players. Americans love a winner. Americans will not tolerate a loser. Americans despise cowards. Americans play to win all of the time. I wouldn't give a hoot in hell for a man who lost and laughed. That's why Americans have never lost nor will ever lose a war; for the very idea of losing is hateful to an American.

To achieve harmony in battle, each weapon must support the other. Team play wins. You "musicians" of Mars must not wait for the band leader to signal to you. You must, each of your own volition, see to it that you come into this concert at the proper time and at the proper place.

All human beings have an innate resistance to obedience. Discipline removes this resistance and, by constant repetition, makes obedience habitual and subconscious.

Battle is an orgy of disorder. No level lawn nor marker flags exist to aid us in strutting ourselves in vain display, but rather groups of weary, wandering men seeking gropingly for means to kill their foes. The sudden change from accustomed

★ ★ ★

The seasoned veterans who had been with General Patton knew he was a stickler for details, such as always wearing helmets and keeping their leggings on. Anyone caught without either could expect a fifty dollar fine. Newcomers—whether enlisted, NCOs or officers—were typically the victims. Old-timers understood that wearing the helmets was a great deterrent to getting nailed by an enemy sniper. Some GIs quipped that they could scratch their head by simply rapping on their steel pot! And, with so many foot ailments plaguing thousands of soldiers—such as trench foot and frostbite—personal hygiene was vital to maintaining a viable fighting force, thus the importance of the leggings to keep socks from getting wet.

order to utter disorder, to chaos, but emphasizes the folly of schooling to precision and obedience where only fierceness and habituated disorder are useful.

We can conquer only by attacking.

It is an unfortunate and, to me, tragic fact that in our attempts to prevent war we have taught our people to belittle the heroic qualities of the soldier. They do not realize that, as Shakespeare put it, the pursuit of "the bubble reputation even at the cannon's mouth" is not only a good military characteristic but also very helpful to the young man when bullets and shells are whistling and crackling around him.

But, what if every man thought that way? Where in the hell would we be now? What would our country, our loved ones, our homes, even the world, be like? No, Goddamn it, Americans don't think like that. Every man does his job. Every man serves the whole. Every department, every unit, is important in the vast scheme of this war. The ordnance men are needed to supply the guns and machinery of war to keep us rolling. The Quartermaster is needed to bring up food and clothes because where we are going there isn't a hell of a lot to steal. Every last man on K.P. has a job to do, even the one who heats our water to keep us from getting the "G.I. Shits."

Remember this; no set piece of tactics is of any merit in itself unless it is executed by heroic and disciplined troops who have self-confidence and who have leaders who take care of them.

Personally, I am of the opinion that older men of experience, who have smelled powder and have been wounded, are of more value than mere youthful exuberance, which has not yet been disciplined. However, I seem to be in the minority in this belief.

When a surgeon decides in the course of an operation to change its objective, to splice that artery or cut deeper and remove another organ which he finds infected, he is not making a snap decision, but one based on years of knowledge, experience and training. It is the same with professional soldiers.

This "Blood and Guts" stuff is quite distasteful to me. I am a very severe disciplinarian because I know that without discipline it is impossible to win battles and that without discipline to send men into battle is to commit murder.

He was the brash gun-slinger, the World War I combatant, wounded in battle, hardened by the prolonged miseries of trench warfare. Patton vowed to never get caught up in another defensive engagement in the next conflict, most likely in Europe, and most likely in the very near future. He trained his troops beyond the breaking point, indifferent to their personal feelings. In 1939 and 1940, large-scale war games were held in Louisiana to test and coordinate the combined forces of the Army, with mixed results. When mounted cavalry forces came up against Patton's armored forces, it was an overwhelming victory for the tankers. (The Nazi blitzkrieg had similar results when they invaded Poland and decimated its highly respected horse cavalry.) Fully believing that only the most disciplined Army would be victorious on the battlefield, Patton honed his "bayonet psychology" to a razor-sharp edge, so that even his enemies feared an encounter with him.

If a man has done his best, what else is there? I consider that I have always done my best. My conscience is clear.

I wish to assure all of my officers and soldiers that I have never and will never criticize them for having done too much. However, I shall certainly relieve them for doing nothing.

Do your duty as you see it, and damn the consequences.

It is the unconquerable soul of man and not the nature of the weapon he uses which insures victory.

Lack of orders is no excuse for inaction. Anything done vigorously is better than nothing done tardily.

My men don't surrender. I don't want to hear of any soldier under my command being captured unless he has been hit. Even if you are hit, you can still fight back. That's not just bull shit either. The kind of man that I want in my command is just like the lieutenant in Libya, who, with a Luger against his chest, jerked off his helmet, swept the gun aside with one hand and busted the hell out of the Kraut with his helmet.

As news of the Nazi blitzkrieg filtered out of Europe, US Army commanders realized they would have to rethink battle strategy to counter such a combined concentration of military might. Army Chief of Staff, General George C. Marshall, moved quickly to establish two armored divisions, with newly promoted Brig. Gen. George Patton as commander of the 2nd Armored Division at Fort Benning in Georgia, eight months before the Japanese attack on Pearl Harbor. Patton's tankers would soon be tested, first at North Africa, then on to Sicily and Italy before rampaging across Fortress Europe, like rolling thunder.

Then he jumped on the gun and went out and killed another German before they knew what the hell was coming off. And, all of that time, this man had a bullet through a lung. There was a real man!

Fame never yet found a man who waited to be found.

If a man does his best, what else is there?

All of the real heroes are not storybook combat fighters, either. Every single man in this Army plays a vital role. Don't ever let up. Don't ever think that your job is unimportant. Every man has a job to do and he must do it. Every man is a vital link in the great chain. What if every truck driver suddenly decided that he didn't like the whine of those shells overhead, turned yellow and jumped headlong into a ditch? The cowardly bastard could say, "Hell, they won't miss me, just one man in thousands."

Genius is an immense capacity for taking pains.

There has been, and is now, a great deal of talk about discipline; but few people, in or out of the Army, know what it is or why it is necessary.

It is absurd to believe that soldiers who cannot be made to wear the proper uniform can be induced to move forward in battle.

Fatigue makes cowards of us all. Men in condition do not tire.

Untutored courage is useless in the face of educated bullets.

There is only one sort of discipline, perfect discipline.

Brave, undisciplined men have no chance against the discipline and valor of other men.

In view of the prevalent opinion in America that soldiers are, of all persons, the least capable of discussing military matters

and that their years of special training is nil compared to the innate military knowledge of lawyers, doctors, and preachers, I am probably guilty of a great heresy in daring to discuss tanks from the viewpoint of a tank officer.

I am firmly convinced that we must have a universal system of training. The only hope for a peaceful world is a powerful America with the adequate means to instantly check aggressors.

Unless we are so armed and prepared, the next war will probably destroy us. No one who has lived in a destroyed country can view such a possibility with anything except horror.

Always do more than is required of you.

The man who finds twenty dollars on the street or wins it at the slot machine thinks lightly of it, and before long it is as lightly spent. The same man who works and sweats for half a week for that same amount respects it and grudgingly parts with it when he has won it. So with patriotism. The light feelings of love and reverence for our country engendered by shouting for the flag on the 4th of July are too haphazard, too cheap. The man who has served a year with sweat and some discomfort feels that truly he has a part in his country, and that of a truth he has, and he is a patriot.

EXCERPT FROM "THE LIFE AND DEATH OF COLONEL GASENOYL" (1944)

T he Life and Death of Colonel Gasenoyl" is a tribute to two of General Patton's fellow officers from the Great War: Colonel Harry Semmes and Colonel Harry "Paddy" Flint, who both distinguished themselves under fire.

Colonel Semmes was in the thick of the fighting, leading an armor unit against Vichy French forces near Morocco in North Africa when his tank was hit several times. He promptly used his anti-tank gun to return the favor and blasted four enemy tanks.

Paddy Flint didn't have armored protection when he confronted Nazi forces at Troina. He boldly stood rock solid, stripped to the waist, smoking a cigarette, and dared the enemy troops to take their best shot, while his own soldiers questioned his sanity. He called out, "Shoot, you bastards, You can't hit me." The Nazi soldiers certainly did their best to accommodate him but all they did was inspire Flint's own soldiers to advance and send them to the hereafter or a POW camp for the duration of the war. (A year later Paddy Flint was shot in the head at close range.) General Patton lost a close friend and wrote "Life and Death . . . " as a tribute.

In Nineteen Hundred and forty-four
  Our land was swept by cruel war
Such parlous times, these halting rhymes
  Can only indicate, no more.

As usual our land defense
  had been cut down to save expense
To a squad or two, which even you'll admit
  is not much armaments.

This paltry force was much despised,
  but the enemy was soon surprised.
For the Cavalry was a sight to see.
  This Cavalry was mechanized!

The soldiers loved old Colonel G.
  No greater man, they thought, than he.
But a soldier's fate was now in wait
  For that mechanical S.O.B.

Oh! What a horrid scene was there,
  Where once had been so brave and fair
Oil and blood were mixed like mud.
  The fumes of gas were everywhere.

But the saddest sight of all to see
  Was the pitiful plight of Colonel G.
A wounded Titan, through with fightin'
  His dying words were, "God damn me!"

Around the turn of the twentieth century, Patton's father taught him a lesson in Viking folklore, that the true heroes were those who died in battle. Prior to every armed conflict, the Valkyrie selected those Norse warriors among them who were worthy of a valiant death. The "chosen ones" could look forward to the afterlife, in Valhalla.

CHAPTER 8

CASUALTIES OF WAR

On the opposite of the road was an endless line of ambulances bringing men back; wounded men. Yet, when the soldiers of the 90th Division saw me, they stood up and cheered.

It was the most moving experience of my life and the knowledge of what the ambulances contained made it still more poignant.

War means fighting and fighting means killing.

Every soldier should realize that casualties in battle are the result of two factors; first, effective enemy fire, and second, the time during which the soldier is exposed to that fire. The enemy's effectiveness in fire is reduced by your fire or by night attacks. The time you are exposed is reduced by the rapidity of your advance.

War is not run on sentiment.

It's God awful. It's terrible, that's what it is. I can see it in a
vision. It comes to haunt me at night. I am standing there

★ ★ ★

*He pushed them hard and required his soldiers to develop a "warrior soul," and if they died in
battle, then they died as heroes. And if they were wounded in battle, General Patton expected
them to have the very best of care. But he also had little tolerance for cowards, those who
feigned psychological trauma or accidentally on purpose shot themselves in the foot to shirk
combat. He would have strung them up if it was his choice, or at least mustered them out of his
unit. In two instances, while visiting field hospitals in Italy, Patton verbally lashed out and
slapped soldiers he felt were less than heroic. Once news got out, he was ordered to apologize to
every man in his command, and then he was reassigned back to England, where he was forced
to wait indefinitely for his next assignment. He just hoped it wouldn't take too long to get back
in the fight to conquer Fortress Europe.*

knee deep in the water and all around me as far as the eye can see are dead men, floating like a school of dynamited fish. They are all floating face up with their eyes wide open and their skins a ghastly white. They are looking at me as they float by and they are saying, "Patton, you bastard, it's your fault. You did this to me. You killed me." I can't stand it, I tell you. By God, I won't go.

One poor fellow had lost his right arm and he cried. Another had lost a leg. All of them were brave and cheerful. A first sergeant who was in for his second wound laughed and said that after he received his third wound he was going to ask to go home. I had told General Marshall months ago that an enlisted man who had been hit three times should be sent home.

The spirit of the men in the Evacuation Hospitals was improving and the incidence of "battle fatigue" and of "self inflicted wounds" had dropped materially. Soldiers like to play on a winning team.

One man had the top of his head blown off and they were just waiting for him to die. He was a horrid bloody mess and was not good to look at or I might develop personal feelings about sending men into battle. That would be fatal for a general.

Audie Murphy was the most decorated GI of the European Campaign and his many awards included the Medal of Honor. In mid-February of 1945, after attending the Medal of Honor ceremony for Lt. James Fields of the 4th Armored Division, General Patton ordered that this new hero NOT return to combat. "It has been my unfortunate observation that whenever a man gets the Medal of Honor or even the Distinguished Service Cross, he usually attempts to outdo himself and gets killed," Patton wrote.

In any war, a commander, no matter what his rank, has to send to certain death, nearly every day, by his own orders, a certain number of men. Some are his personal friends. All are his personal responsibility; to them as his troops and to their families. Any man with a heart would like to sit down and bawl like a baby, but he can't. So, he sticks out his jaw, and swaggers and swears. I wish some of those pious sob sisters at home could understand something as basic as that.

★ ★ ★

You are not all going to die. Only two percent of you right here today would die in a major battle. Death must not be feared.

DEAD PALS (1919)

Dickey, we've trained and fit and died,
Yes, drilled and drunk and bled,
and shared our chuck and our bunks in life.
Why part us now we're dead?

Would I rot so nice away from you,
Who has been my pal for a year?
Will Gabriel's trumpet waken me,
If you ain't there to hear?

Will a parcel of bones in a wooden box
Remind my Ma of me?
Or isn't it better for her to think
Of the kid I used to be?

It's true some preacher will get much class
A tellin' what guys we've been,
So, the fact that we're not sleeping with pals,
Won't cut no ice for him.

They'll yell, "Hurrah!"
and every spring they'll decorate our tomb,
But we'll be absent at the spot
We sought, and found, our doom.

The flags and flowers won't bother us,
Our free souls will be far—
Holdin' the line in sunny France
Where we died to win the war.

Fact is, we need no flowers and flags
For each peasant will tell his son,
"Them graves on the hill is the graves of
Yanks, Who died to lick the Hun."

And instead of comin' every spring
To squeeze a languid tear,
A friendly people's loving care
Will guard us all the year.

* * *

George Patton was a learned man, a student of warfare, who could recite verbatim lengthy quotes from those leaders who inspired him to greatness:

> "Whoever of you has wounds, let him strip and show them, and I will show mine in turn; for there is no part of my body . . . remaining free from wounds, nor is there any kind of weapon used either for close combat or for hurling at the enemy, the traces of which I do not bear on my person. For I have been wounded with the sword in close fight, I have been shot with arrows, and I have been hit with missiles projected from engines of war, and though often times I have been hit with stones and bolts of wood for the sake of your lives, your glory and your wealth, I am still leading you as conquerors over all the land and sea, all rivers, mountains and plains."

(Alexander the Great)

TO OUR FIRST DEAD (1918)

They died for France
like countless thousands more
Who, in this war, have faltered not to go
At duty's bidding, even unto death.
and yet, no deaths which history records,

Were fought with greater consequence
than theirs.
A nation shuddered as their spirits passed;
and unborn babies trembled in the womb,
In sympathetic anguish at their fate.

Far from their homes and in ungainful strife
They gave their all, in that they gave their life;
While their young blood,
shed in this distant land,
Shall be more potent than the dragon's teeth

To raise up soldiers to avenge their fall.
Men talked of sacrifice, but there was none;
Death found them unafraid and free to come
Before their God. In righteous battle slain
A joyous privilege theirs; the first to go
In that their going doomed to certain wrath
A thousand foemen, for each drop they gave
Of sacramental crimson, to the cause.

And so their youthful forms all dank and stiff,
All stained with tramplings in unlovely mud,
We laid to rest beneath the soil of France
So often honored with the hero slain;

Yet never greatlier so than on this day,
When we interred our first dead in her heart.
There let them rest,
wrapped in her verdant arms,
Their task well done.

Now, from the smoke veiled sky,
They watch our khaki legions
pass to certain victory,
Because of them who showed us how to die.

★ ★ ★

"All the men steal looks at me . . . it is complimentary but a
little terrible. I am their God or so they seem to think."
(Patton diary entry, July 3, 1943)

CHAPTER 9

GOD OF BATTLES

GOD OF BATTLES (1943)

From pride and foolish confidence,
From every weakening creed,
From the dread fear of fearing,
Protect us, Lord and lead.

Great God, who, through the ages,
Has braced the bloodstained hand,
As Saturn, Jove, or Woden
Has led our Warrior band.

Again we seek thy counsel,
But not in cringing guise,
We whine not for thy mercy,
To slay; God make us wise.

For slaves who shun the issue
  Who do not ask thy aid,
    To Thee we trust our spirits,
      Our bodies, unafraid.

From doubt and fearsome boding
  Still Thou our spirits guard,
    Make strong our souls to conquer.
      Give us the victory, Lord.

It is foolish and wrong to mourn the men who died. Rather we should thank God that such men lived.

This war makes higher demands on courage and discipline than any war of which I have known. But, when you see men who have demonstrated discipline and courage, killed and wounded, it naturally raises a lump in your throat and sometimes produces a tear in your eye.

The only way for a soldier to die is by the last bullet of the last battle of his last war.

The pacifist actually refuses to defend what defends him; his country. In the final analysis this is the most basic immoral position.

The greatest privilege of citizenship is to be able to freely bear arms under one's country's flag.

No sane man is not afraid in battle, but discipline produces in him a form of vicarious courage which, with his manhood, makes for victory. Self-respect grows directly from discipline. The Army saying, "Whoever saw a dirty soldier with a medal?" is largely true. Pride, in turn, stems from self-respect and from the knowledge that the soldier is an American.

THE STRATEGY OF RAPID ADVANCE

The Nazis may have developed the steamroller strategy known as blitzkrieg—with the combined forces of infantry, artillery, armor, and aviation all converging on the battlefront, to overwhelm and overrun the enemy with devastating firepower—but General Patton perfected it and unleashed it against the German army.

> We must keep moving. Do not sit down. Do not say, "I have done enough." Always see what else you can do to raise hell with the enemy. You must have a desperate determination to continually go forward.

In case of doubt, ATTACK!

A good solution applied with vigor now is better than a perfect solution applied ten minutes later.

A good plan violently executed right now is far better than a perfect plan executed next week.

People must try to use their imagination. When orders fail to come they must act on their own best judgment. A very safe rule to follow is that in case of doubt, push on a little further and then keep on pushing.

★ ★ ★

9th Armored Division forces rush to Bastogne to punch through the Nazi lines surrounding American forces in the embattled city.

Speed and ruthless violence on the beaches is vital. There must be no hesitation in debarking. To linger on the beaches is fatal.

Americans pride themselves on being He Men and they ARE He Men. Remember that the enemy is just as frightened as you are and probably more so. They are not supermen. All through your Army careers, you men have bitched about what you call "chicken shit drilling." That, like everything else in this Army, has a definite purpose. That purpose

is alertness. Alertness must be bred into every soldier. I don't give a f*** for a man who's not always on his toes. You men are veterans or you wouldn't be here. You are ready for what's to come. A man must be alert at all times if he expects to stay alive. If you're not alert, sometime, a German son-of-an-asshole-bitch is going to sneak up behind you and beat you to death with a sockful of shit!"

And you should have seen those trucks on the road to Tunisia. Those drivers were magnificent. All day and all night they rolled over those son-of-a-bitching roads, never stopping, never faltering from their course, with shells bursting all around them all of the time. We got through on good old American guts. Many of those men drove for over forty consecutive hours. These men weren't combat men, but they were soldiers with a job to do. They did it and in one hell of a way they did it. They were part of a team. Without team effort, without them, the fight would have been lost. All of the links in the chain pulled together and the chain became unbreakable.

You don't have to hurry, you have to run like hell.

Now if you are going to win any battle you have to do one thing. You have to make the mind run the body. Never let the body tell the mind what to do. The body will always give up. It is always tired morning, noon, and night. But the body is never tired if the mind is not tired. When you were younger the mind could make you dance all night, and the body was never tired . . . You've always got to make the mind take over and keep going.

★ ★ ★

The night attack was interesting, because they had to advance through a mine field. They chose to do it in the dark and, as a result, lost 35 men. Had they advanced in the daytime, they would probably have lost the same 35 men to mines and, in addition, several hundred men to machine gun and rifle fire.

The Americans as a race are the greatest mechanic in the world. America as a nation has the greatest ability for mass production of machines. It therefore behooves us to devise methods of war which exploit our inherent superiority. We must fight the war by machines on the ground and in the air to the maximum of our ability.

History is replete with accounts of military inventions, each heralded by its disciples as the "Dernier Cri"—the "Key" to victory.

A tank which stops to fire, gets hit.

. . . a tank fight is just like a barroom fight—the fellow who gets the hit wins. Our men, especially in the 4th Armored, are magnificent shots. The 4th, 2nd and 3rd Armored are old divisions and have plenty of practice. I used to train them to get on a target of 30 degrees off target in three seconds. They did not do it, but they got awfully fast.

. . . the whole thing in tank fighting is to train crews not
as individuals but as crews.

American soldiers are most ingenious. When they could
not capture a town to sleep in, they would roll three large

*Like shooting fish in a barrel, enemy machine gunners, mortar, and artillery crews could
simply wait till the invasion beaches were clogged with thousands of Allied soldiers plus all the
weaponry and accoutrements they needed to wage war, then the Nazi defenders could open up
with a barrage of hot metal.*

*George Patton was adamant that his forces not gather in any one place for too long, such
as landing beaches, and allow the Nazis to move their heavy guns into position. He wanted
them on the move, always forward, often directly into enemy fire, but somehow someone would
break through and neutralize their tormentors, thus allowing the follow-on units to push
inland.*

snowballs or snow rolls, place one on each side and the third on the windward end, and, lining them with pine tree branches, they slept in groups of three or four. How human beings could endure this continuous fighting at sub-zero temperatures is still beyond my comprehension.

Success in war depends on the "golden rules of war"; speed, simplicity, and boldness.

Looking over the country where we fought during the battle of El Guettar gives one a definite idea of the greatness of the American soldier. The mountains are impossibly difficult. Had I known how difficult it was, I might have been less bold—but it is always well to remember that the country is just as hard on the enemy as it is on you.

As long as you attack them, they cannot find the time to attack you.

Take calculated risks. That is quite different from being rash.

★ ★ ★

Sometimes the advance was seventy miles a day. Or it might only be seventy yards as they went house by house, floor by floor.

And on really bad days, their advance might be measured in inches . . . and lives lost. By far, the worst of the worst was trying to neutralize the Germans holding out at Metz, a heavily fortified city in the Alsace-Lorraine region of France. Patton was not a proponent of defensive positions, but Metz, with its thick walls, bunkers, trenches, and tunnels, built to withstand any foolhardy frontal attacks and aerial bombardments, would test his patience during late 1944.

Nobody ever defended anything successfully, there is only attack and attack and attack some more.

★ ★ ★

The tank must be used boldly. It is new and always has the element of surprise. It is also terrifying to look at as the infantry soldier is helpless before it.

★ ★ ★

"Soldiers of the Seventh Army: Born at sea, baptized in blood and crowned with victory, in the course of 38 days of incessant battle and unceasing labor, you have added a glorious chapter to the history of war."

—*August 22, 1943*

SEVEN UP

General Patton's poems are graphically brutal, intensely personal, conveying his feelings, his visions of the moment at hand, the moment that prompted him to rip open a vein and bleed his heart out on paper. They may not be able to withstand the harsh glare of literary critique, but his verses do reveal small glimpses of this complex man who exuded surliness and rarely displayed his softer side.

"Seven Up" refers to the mighty Seventh Army and its five-week campaign of Sicily. Soon after, Patton was removed from command after he slapped two soldiers he felt were feigning cowardice in field hospitals. While writing this poem, he felt that one day he would once again lead the Seventh to more conquests. Instead, he would head up the Third Army in the final battles of Fortress Europe.

SEVEN UP (1943)

Once there was an Army,
*   then one day it died.*
So tell the bell and waken Hell,
*   to give it room inside.*

The story of this Army
*   is very, very drear*
Its beginning and its ending
*   were especially queer.*

They made its chief a permanent
*   so he perchance could wave*
At others hurrying past him
*   their country for to save.*

But now just like a skeleton
*   upon the desert floor*
Orders like vultures come each day
*   to pick away some more*

The thing has got so very bad
*   that now his friends suspect*
That he no longer can command
*   even his self-respect.*

Yet like the fabled Phoenix
*   The Seventh shall arise*
Again to soar in triumph
*   through flaming smoke veiled skies.*

With his son at West Point, Patton gave him some fatherly advice on June 6, 1944: "What you must know is how man reacts. Weapons change, but man who uses them changes not at all. To win battles you do not beat weapons . . . you beat the soul of the enemy." That "soul" was the individual soldier, and Patton truly believed the American GI was better than any combatant he would face in battle.

★ ★ ★

General Patton had a simple solution for resolving the war with Nazi Germany: a head-to-head confrontation with his chief adversary, Field Marshal Erwin Rommel, commander of the Afrika Korps, with German and Allied soldiers watching from a safe distance. Like the knights of yore, they would fight to the death, winner take all, and their weapons of choice would be . . . tanks, one on one.

CHAPTER 12

THOSE NAZI BASTARDS

The only thing to do when a son of a bitch looks cross-eyed at you is to beat the hell out of him right then and there.

We are going to kill German bastards. I would prefer to skin them alive, but gentlemen, I fear some of our people at home would accuse me of being too rough.

No poor bastard ever won a war by dying for his country. He won it by making other bastards die for their country.

We'll win this war, but we'll win it only by fighting and by showing the Germans that we've got more guts than they have; or ever will have. We're not going to just shoot the sons-of-bitches, we're going to rip out their living

Goddamned guts and use them to grease the treads of our
tanks. We're going to murder those lousy Hun cocksuckers
by the bushel-f***ing-basket. War is a bloody, killing business.
You've got to spill their blood, or they will spill yours. Rip
them up the belly. Shoot them in the guts. When shells are
hitting all around you and you wipe the dirt off your face and
realize that instead of dirt it's the blood and guts of what
once was your best friend beside you, you'll know what to do!

May God have mercy upon my enemies, because I won't.

At midnight on the night of December 31st, 1944 all guns in the Third Army fired rapid fire for twenty minutes on the Germans as a New Year's greeting. When the firing ceased, our forward observers stated they could hear the Germans screaming in the woods.

I don't want to get any messages saying, "I am holding my position." We are not holding a Goddamned thing. Let the

General Patton thrived in the spotlight, in the thick of combat. His only rival on the far side of the battlefield was Germany's own armor commander, Erwin Rommel, who later wrote, "We had to wait until the Patton Army was in France to see the most astonishing achievements in mobile warfare."

Each of these tacticians studied and respected their opponent, though they never actually faced one another. Patton relished nothing better than to take on Rommel, man to man, tank versus tank, anytime, anywhere.

Germans do that. We are advancing constantly and we are
not interested in holding onto anything, except the enemy's
balls. We are going to twist his balls and kick the living shit
out of him all of the time. Our basic plan of operation is
to advance and to keep on advancing regardless of whether
we have to go over, under, or through the enemy. We are

★ ★ ★

*"Sure, we want to go home. We want this war over with. The quickest way to get it over with
is to go get the bastards who started it. The quicker they are whipped, the quicker we can go
home. The shortest way home is through Berlin and Tokyo. And when we get to Berlin, I am
personally going to shoot that paper hanging son-of-a-bitch Hitler. Just like I'd shoot a snake!"*

—*Patton addressing his troops before Operation Overlord, June 5, 1944*

going to go through him like crap through a goose; like shit through a tin horn!

I have studied the German all of my life. I have read the memoirs of his generals and political leaders. I have even read his philosophers and listened to his music. I have studied in detail the accounts of every damned one of his battles. I know exactly how he will react under any given set of circumstances. He hasn't the slightest idea of what I'm going to do. Therefore, when the time comes, I'm going to whip the Hell out of him.

All Nazis are bad, but not all Germans are Nazis.

* * *

I consider it no sacrifice to die for my country. In my mind, we came here to thank God that men like these have lived rather than to regret that they have died.

* * *

The Nazis came to power in 1933 and Adolf Hitler immediately set out to violate or ignore every term of the Versailles Treaty, which ended World War I. This included a massive armaments buildup that gave Germany the military muscle to threaten surrounding countries and regions, allowing them to add "living space" in Hitler's quest to create a Thousand Year Reich.

By the time the United States officially entered the war in late 1941, Nazi Germany had perfected its weaponry and honed its battle tactics, resulting in an all-encompassing, overpowering show of force they dubbed Blitzkrieg.

US military leaders understood that Nazi Germany would be a formidable foe and they would have to scrap the trench warfare tactics from World War I and develop new strategies with equally devastating effect.

★ ★ ★

The last thing "Blood and Guts" Patton wanted was a high casualty count among his men. (He certainly didn't mind obliterating Nazi forces at every opportunity.) He knew there was a direct correlation between rapid advance and minimal losses, and so he constantly badgered his commanders to maintain the offensive, to take on the enemy with brutality, with ruthlessness, with no room for compassion.

From time to time there will be some complaints that we are pushing our people too hard. I don't give a good Goddamn about such complaints. I believe in the old and sound rule that an ounce of sweat will save a gallon of blood. The harder WE push, the more Germans we will kill. The more Germans we kill, the fewer of our men will be killed. Pushing means fewer casualties. I want you all to remember that.

---

* * *

The Nazi hierarchy, (including Adolf Hitler, who dictated much of the military actions in World War II), realized George Patton was "the gravest and most immediate threat" wherever he led Allied combat forces. As such, the German High Command attempted to track his every move and fortify their positions along the battlefront in anticipation of his forward thrust.

There are four hundred neatly marked graves somewhere in Sicily, all because one man went to sleep on the job. But they are German graves, because we caught the bastard asleep before they did. An Army is a team. It lives, sleeps, eats and fights as a team. This individual heroic stuff is pure horse shit. The bilious bastards who write that kind of stuff for the *Saturday Evening Post* don't know any more about real fighting under fire than they know about f(ornicat)ing!

★ ★ ★

If he had his way, Patton would have killed every Nazi soldier, but even officers in defeat were accorded decent treatment.

We have the finest food, the finest equipment, the best spirit and the best men in the world. Why, by God, I actually pity those poor sons-of-bitches we're going up against. By God, I do.

Don't forget, you men don't know that I'm here. No mention of that fact is to be made in any letters. The world is not supposed to know what the hell happened to me. I'm not supposed to be commanding this Army. I'm not even supposed to be here in England. Let the first bastards to find out be the Goddamned Germans. Someday I want to see them raise up on their piss-soaked hind legs and howl, "Jesus Christ, it's the Goddamned Third Army again and that son-of-a-bitch Patton."

We want to get the hell over there. The quicker we clean up
this Goddamned mess, the quicker we can take a little jaunt
against the purple pissing Japs and clean out their nest, too.
Before the Goddamned Marines get all of the credit.

★ ★ ★

There were very few sympathetic souls on the battlefield. It was kill or be killed. General Patton wanted skirmishes with the enemy to be brutal and at lightning speed, and he preferred that all the dying be done by the enemy, with the victors taking whatever "souvenirs" they wished.

★ ★ ★

When a man is lying in a shell hole, if he just stays there all day, a German will get to him eventually. The hell with that idea. The hell with taking it. My men don't dig foxholes. I don't want them to. Foxholes only slow up an offensive. Keep moving. And don't give the enemy time to dig one either.

CHAPTER 13

A SOLDIER'S PRAYER

A SOLDIER'S PRAYER (1944)

God of our Fathers, who by land and sea has ever led us on to victory, please continue your inspiring guidance in this greatest of our conflicts.

Strengthen my soul so that the weakening instinct of self preservation, which besets all of us in battle, shall not blind me to my duty to my own manhood, to the Glory of my calling, and to my responsibility to my Fellow soldiers.

Grant to our Armed Forces that disciplined valor and mutual confidence which insures success in war. Let me not mourn for the men who have died fighting, but rather let me be glad that such heroes have lived. If it be my lot to die,

let me do so with courage and honor in a
manner which will bring the greatest harm to the
enemy, please, oh Lord, protect and guide those
I shall leave behind. Give us victory, Lord.

★ ★ ★

Burial of the dead was not a pleasant affair and often temporary cemeteries were created until the bodies could be recovered and returned home. In his many writings, George Patton made cutting references to temporary graves: he didn't want soldiers to dig slit trenches along tree lines and sleep in them because, if the enemy unleashed an artillery barrage, the splintered tree branches would impale those prone soldiers which would only be "of some assistance to the graves registration people."

He also didn't want cemeteries located along avenues of advance, "where they can be seen by replacements marching to the front. This has a very bad effect on morale, even if it adds to the pride of the graves registration service."

★ ★ ★

George Patton had numerous influences, rooted in the centuries-old tales of bold leaders whose legacies are etched in stone.

"He was very clear in recognizing what was necessary to be done, even when it was a matter still unnoticed by others; and very successful in conjecturing from the observation of facts what was likely to occur. In marshalling, arming and ruling an army he was exceedingly skillful; and very renowned for rousing the courage of his soldiers, filling them with hopes of success, and dispelling their fear in the midst of danger by his own freedom of fear" (Arrian writing about Alexander the Great).

Patton disliked the moniker "Old Blood and Guts," but he was also referred to as "Flash Gordon" and "the Green Hornet." Of course there were a few other choice nicknames said behind his back, but what he liked to hear the most was simply, "Sir."

CHAPTER 14

THE UNITY OF COMMAND

There must be one commander for ground, air and sea. The trouble is that we lack leaders with sufficient strength of character. I could do it and possibly will. As I gain experience, I do not think more of myself, but less of others. Men, even so called great men, are wonderfully weak and timid. They are too damned polite.

Sometimes I think that I am not such a great commander after all; just a fighting animal.

There is a great deal of talk about loyalty from the bottom to the top. Loyalty from the top down is even more necessary and is much less prevalent. One of the most frequently noted characteristics of great men who have remained great is loyalty to their subordinates.

★ ★ ★

They all get scared and then I appear and they feel better.

———————— ★ ★ ★ ————————

Thousands of Allied soldiers were crammed onto transport ships for the journey from England's southern shores to the French coast of Normandy on June 5, 1944. Thousands more were held back in reserve. One of them was particularly perturbed that he was left out of the biggest offensive of the century. General George Patton was being used instead to dupe the Nazis into thinking he was heading up Armegruppe Patton, the main invasion force that would traverse the short distance across the Channel and storm ashore at Calais, where the bulk of the Nazis waited. On June 6, as Allied troops hit the beaches at Normandy, German forces at Calais waited . . . for the invasion that never happened.

I have a notion that usually the great things a man does appear to be great only after we have passed them. When they are at hand they are normal decisions and are done without knowledge. In the case of a General, for example, the almost superhuman knowledge which he is supposed to possess exists only in the mind of his biographer.

A piece of spaghetti or a military unit can only be led from the front end.

The greatest gift a general can have is a bad temper. A bad temper gives you a sort of divine wrath and it is only by the use of a divine wrath that you can drive men beyond their physical ability in order to save their lives.

War is simple, direct, and ruthless. It takes a simple, direct, and ruthless man to wage it.

Goddammit, I'm not running for the Shah of Persia. There are no practice games in life. It's eat or be eaten, kill or be killed. I want my bunch to be in there first, to be the "firstest with the mostest."

They won't do it if I ask them nicely.

As usual on the verge of action, everyone felt full of doubt except myself. It has always been my unfortunate role to be the ray of sunshine and the backslapper before action, both for those under me and also those over me.

I am a soldier, I fight where I am told, and I win where I fight.

People ask why I swagger and swear, wear flashy uniforms and sometimes two pistols. Well, I'm not sure whether or not some of it isn't my own fault. However that may be, the press and others have built a picture of me. So, now, no matter how tired, or discouraged, or really even ill I may be, if I don't live up to that picture, my men are going to say, "The old man's sick, the old son of a bitch has had it." Then their own confidence, their own morale will take a big drop.

. . . it is always best, where practical, to drive to the front, so that the soldiers can see you going in that direction, and to

★ ★ ★

---

*He was the Supreme Commander for Allied forces in Europe and prior to ordering the inva-
sion of France, General Dwight D. Eisenhower visited with the troops massing in southern
England.*

*As a peripheral part of Operation Overlord, Ike ordered General George Patton to head up
a fictitious task force, in order to confuse the Nazis deployed along the French coast, primarily
at Calais, the closest point to England. By nightfall of June 6, 1944, with thousands of Allied
troops ashore at Normandy, the Nazis still felt it was a diversion, and so they waited and continued to wait for the much-feared George Patton and his tidal wave to make his move.*

save time, fly back by Cub plane so that you are never seen going to the rear.

There are apparently two types of successful soldiers. Those who get on by being unobtrusive and those who get on by being obtrusive. I am of the latter type and seem to be rare and unpopular, but it is my method.

I am probably the most unpopular man, not only in the 2nd Armored Division, but in the whole Army. I get very tired of being the only person in this outfit who makes any corrections.

The more I see of the so called great, the less they impress me. I am better.

When I think of the greatness of my job, and realize that I am what I am, I am amazed. But, on reflection, who is as good as I am? I know of no one.

Truly, for so fierce a warrior, I have a damned mild expression.

I can't see how people can be so dull and lacking in imagination. Compared to them I am a genius. I think I am.

War is the only place where a man lives.

I have trained myself so that usually I can keep right on talking when an explosion occurs quite close. I take a sly pleasure in seeing others bat their eyes or look around.

I am scared, but I still want to get to the front.

I still get scared under fire. I guess I never will get used to it, but I still poke along.

★ ★ ★

I drove to Trier via Wasservillig. The Roman Legions marching on Trier from Luxembourg used this same road, and one could almost smell the coppery sweat and see the low dust clouds where those stark fighters moved forward into battle. As a memorial to their great deeds, the least demolished

building standing in Trier was the gateway to the Roman amphitheater.

All very successful commanders are prima donnas and must be so treated.

Accept the challenges so that you can feel the exhilaration of victory.

★ ★ ★

Use steamroller strategy; that is, make up your mind on
course and direction of action and stick to it. But in tactics,
do not steamroller. Attack weakness. Hold them by the nose
and kick them in the ass.

★ ★ ★

*"His life was the stride of a demi-god, from battle to battle and from victory to victory," wrote
J. W. von Goethe, on Napoleon Bonaparte.*

*"What distinguishes (him) the most is not his skill in maneuvering, but his audacity. He
carried out things I never dared to do," stated Napoleon about Frederick the Great.*

*Both of these revered leaders could also have been referring to George Patton, who truly
believed he was destined to create a lasting legacy as a great warrior, one who would be
studied and critiqued and talked about for generations to come: ". . . I believe that one's spirit
enlarges with responsibility and that, with God's help, I shall make (momentous decisions)
and make them right. When this job is done, I presume I will be pointed to the next step in the
ladder of destiny. If I do my full duty, the rest will take care of itself" (Diary entry, November
6, 1942).*

It is hard to answer intelligently the question, "Why I want to be a soldier." For my own satisfaction I have tried to give myself reasons but have never found any logical ones. I only feel that it is inside me. It is as natural for me to be a soldier as it is to breathe and would be as hard to give up all thought of being a soldier as it would be to stop breathing.

I am not a brilliant soldier. So far, I have been quite successful because I am always fully confident that I can do what must be done and have had my sense of duty developed to the point where I let no personal interests or danger interfere.

Among leaders of whatever rank there are three types; 10% genius, 80% average and 10% fools. The average group is the critical element in battle. It is better to give such men several simple alternative solutions which, by repeated practice, they can independently apply than it is to attempt to think for them via the ever-fallible means of communication.

★ ★ ★

The duties of an officer are the safety, honor and welfare of your country first; the honor, welfare, and comfort of the men in your command second; and the officer's own ease, comfort, and safety last.

In my opinion, we will only win this war through blood, sacrifice, and courage. In order to get willing fighters, we must develop the highest possible "Esprit de Corps." Therefore, the removal of distinctive badges and insignia from the uniform is highly detrimental. To die willingly, as many of us must, we must have tremendous pride not only in our nation and in ourselves, but also in the unit to which we belong.

The important thing in any organization is the creation of a soul, which is based on pride, in the unit.

The flag is to the patriot what the cross is to the Christian.

There are more tired Corps and Division commanders than there are tired Corps and Divisions.

The hardest thing a general has to do is to wait for the battle to start after all of the orders have been given.

Civilization has affected us. We abhor personal encounter.
Many a man will risk his life, with an easy mind, in a burning
house who would recoil from having his nose punched. We
have been taught restraint from our emotions, to look upon
anger as low, until many of us have never experienced the
God sent ecstasy of unbridled wrath. We have never felt our

*George Patton had little use for armchair generals or those who made decisions based on
diplomacy, and so he was frequently at odds with his counterparts and his superiors, such as
Eisenhower and Bradley, two highly respected leaders, each with his own way of getting the
job done. They both knew Patton was the best war fighter in the European Campaign—"no
other commander could match him in reckless haste and boldness," Bradley recalled—but they
kept him on a very short leash. Naturally Patton made every effort to gnaw free so he could do
what they wanted him to do, what he was destined to do.*

eyes screw up, our temples throb, and have never had the red mist gather in our sight. But, we expect that a man shall, in an instant, in the twinkling of an eye, divest himself of all restraint, of all caution, and hurl himself upon the enemy, a frenzied beast, lusting to probe his enemy's guts with three feet of steel or to shatter his brain with a bullet.

Gentlemen, it cannot be done without mental practice. Therefore, you must school yourselves to savagery. You must imagine how it will feel when your sword hilt crashes into the breastbone of your enemy. You must picture the wild exaltation of the mounted charge when the lips are drawn back into a snarl and the voice cracks with a passion. At one time, you must be both a wise man and a fool.

I guess that I am the only one who sees glory in war.

Magnificent! Compared to war, all other forms of human endeavor shrink to insignificance. God help me, I do love it so!

All glory is fleeting.

A young soldier upon being asked by Napoleon what he desired in recompense for an heroic act said, "Sire, the

Legion of Honor," to which Napoleon replied, "My boy, you are over young for such an honor." The soldier again said, "Sire, in your service, we do not grow old."

This story is as true as it is tragic. Our men do not grow old. We must exploit their abilities and satisfy their longings to the utmost during the brief span of their existence. Surely, an inch of satin for a machine gun nest put out of action is a bargain not to be lightly passed up.

Who ever saw a dirty soldier with a medal?

A CODE OF ACTION (1917)

I didn't begin with askings
I took my job and stuck
I took the chances they wouldn't
and now they are calling it luck.

In wondrous catlike ability
For grasping all things which go by
To land on my feet with agility
No one is greater than I.

In doing the things others will not
In standing the blows others shirk
In grasping the chance that returns not
and never yet shirking my work.

For these gifts, Oh! God, I thank Thee
Pray let me continue the same
Since, by doing things well which are nearest
Perhaps I shall yet rise to fame.

It is not in intricate planning
Nor yet in regretting the past
That great men whose lives we are watching
Have gained to their greatness at last.

Hence praise we the just mead of striving
Which foolish make light of as luck
There never was yet luck in shirking
While much is accomplished through pluck.

So seize I the things which are nearest
and studious fall on my feet
Do ever in all things my damndest
and never, Oh, never retreat!

I visited the troops near Coutances and found an armored division sitting on a road, while its headquarters, secreted behind an old church, was deeply engrossed in the study of maps, I asked why they had not crossed the Seine. They told me they were making a study of it at the moment, but could not find such a place and was informed that they were studying the map to that end.

I then told them I had just waded across it, that it was
not over two feet deep, and that the only defense I knew
about was one machine gun which had fired very inaccurately
at me. I repeated the Japanese proverb—"One look is worth
one hundred reports"—and asked them why in hell they had
not gone down to the river personally.

Commanding an army is not such a very absorbing task
except that one must be ready at all hours of the day and
night to make some momentous decision, which frequently
consists of telling somebody who thinks that he is beaten
that he is not beaten.

I continued to walk up and down the beachhead and soon
shamed them into getting up and fighting.

It is really amazing what the determination on the part of
one man can do to many thousands.

Wars may be fought with weapons, but they are won by men.
It is the spirit of the men who follow and the man who leads
that gains victory.

While waiting in England to get back into the fight, Patton oversaw the build-up of Fortitude South, which was little more than a full array of trucks and tanks and artillery pieces made of rubber, docks and wharves, empty hangars, and barracks made of plywood, and flimsy landing craft and harbor equipment which all resembled the real things, at least from a distance, if viewed by enemy surveillance planes and spies roaming southern England.

Nazi cryptologists monitored radio traffic for any nuggets related to the forthcoming invasion of mainland Europe, most likely at Calais, a mere twenty miles from the English coast.

Knowing his every move and comment was being scrutinized, General Patton issued an address to all of the combatants involved with Operation Overlord:

Excerpt from General Patton's Address to the Troops

General George S. Patton Jr.
Before the commencement of Operation Overlord.
Somewhere in England.

Men, this stuff that some sources sling around about America wanting out of this war, not wanting to fight, is a crock of bullshit. Americans love to fight, traditionally. All real Americans love the sting and clash of battle. You are here today for three reasons. First, because you are here to defend your homes and your loved ones. Second, you are here for your own self respect, because you would not want to be anywhere else. Third, you are here because you are real men and all real men like to fight.

Send a gasoline can to Montgomery with this message; "Although I am sadly short of gasoline myself, I know of your admiration for our equipment and supplies and I can spare you this five gallons. It will be more than enough to take you as far as you probably will advance in the next two days."

★ ★ ★

While other Allied commanders leaned toward the slow and methodical approach to warfare, George Patton wanted to throw lightning bolts, get the Nazi forces on the run and keep on pushing them, all the way back to Berlin. When British commander Bernard Montgomery complained to Eisenhower that Patton was moving too fast and thus requiring more than his fair share of gasoline to keep his tanks moving, Ike ordered Patton to halt, and wait for Monty. It was inconceivable that a lack of fuel—his tanks needed four hundred thousand gallons every day—could stall the advance, allowing the Nazis time to regroup and possibly go back on the offensive.

Go until the last shot is fired and the last drop of gasoline is gone. Then go forward on foot.

Better to fight for something than live for nothing.

The more senior the officer, the more time he has to go to the front.

There is nothing harsh in brief words of command any more than there is impoliteness in the brief wording of a telegram. Commands simply express your desire, your signal, in the briefest and most emphatic language possible. If you are to obtain obedience from your men, your language must express your meaning concisely and with emphasis. Further, each meaning must always be expressed in precisely the same language. In this way, when you give commands in battle, the unreasoning mind of the soldier will automatically carry out the set of instructions to which he has become accustomed. It is inexcusable for you to express yourself in an ambiguous or hesitating manner.

★ ★ ★

A man of diffident manner will never inspire confidence. A cold reserve cannot beget enthusiasm.

Never tell people how to do things. Tell them what to do and they will surprise you with their ingenuity.

★ ★ ★

Patton blamed his biggest obstacle—Montgomery—for prolonging the war in Europe by at least six months, allowing the Nazis to regroup, clandestinely reposition their forces, and launch the last-ditch Battle of the Bulge during the winter of 1944.

A leader is a man who can adapt principles to circumstances.

I prefer a loyal staff officer to a brilliant one.

There is nothing more pathetic and futile than a general who lives long enough to explain a defeat.

There has been a great deal of talk about loyalty from the bottom to the top. Loyalty from the top to the bottom is much more important, and also much less prevalent. It is this loyalty from the top to the bottom which binds juniors to their seniors with the strength of steel.

Do your damnedest in an ostentatious manner all the time.

If everyone is thinking alike, then somebody isn't thinking.
    Officers must assert themselves by example and by voice.

There is no "approved" solution to any tactical situation.

If a man thinks war long enough, it is bound to have a good effect on him.

There is a fine line between combat and religion. Men trained as warriors want nothing more than peace, but sometimes it requires brutality to rid the world of dictators such as Adolf Hitler. Going into battle, soldiers on both sides pray to the same God, but he rarely chooses sides.

George Patton noted the dilemma soon after his forces made it to France: "The first Sunday I spent in Normandy was quite impressive. I went to a Catholic Field Mass where all of us were armed. As we knelt in the mud in the slight drizzle, we could distinctly hear the roar of the guns, and the whole sky was filled with airplanes on their missions of destruction . . . quite at variance with the teachings of the religion we were practicing."

Never make excuses whether or not it is your fault.

Re-grouping is the curse of war and it is a great boon to the enemy.

It may be of interest to future generals to realize that one makes plans to fit the circumstances, and does not try to create circumstances to fit plans.

Success demands a high level of logistical and organizational competence.

If I do my full duty, the rest will take care of itself.

Leadership is the thing that wins battles. I have it, but I'll be damned if I can define it. It probably consists of knowing what you want to do, and then doing it and getting mad as hell if anyone tries to get in your way. Self confidence and leadership are twin brothers.

★ ★ ★

"When I was a little boy at home, I used to wear a wooden sword and say to myself, 'George S. Patton Jr., Lieutenant General.' At that time I did not know there were full generals. Now I want, and will get, four stars," Patton recalled after getting his third star and taking over II Corps in March of 1943.

Be willing to make decisions. That's the most important quality in a good leader.

The time to take counsel of your fears is before you make an important battle decision. That's the time to listen to every fear you can imagine! When you have collected all the facts and fears and made your decision, turn off all your fears and go ahead!

. . . Whether these tactical thoughts of mine are the result of inspiration or insomnia, I have never been able to determine, but nearly every tactical idea I had ever had has come into my head full-born, much after the manner of Minerva from the head of Jupiter.

I think that it is worthy to note that the primary function of an Armored Force is to disrupt command, communications, and supply.

Strategy and tactics do not change. The means only of applying them differ.

CONQUERING INNER TURMOILS

FEAR (1945)

I am that dreadful, blighting thing,
  Like rat holes to the flood.
    Like rust that gnaws the faultless blade,
      Like microbes to the blood.

I know no mercy and no truth,
  The young I blight, the old I slay.
    Regret stalks darkly in my wake,
      and ignominy dogs my way.

Sometimes, in virtuous garb I rove,
  With facile talk of easier way;
    Seducing where I dare not rape,
      Young manhood, from its honor's sway.

★ ★ ★

War is ugly and George Patton made no attempt to sanitize the ugliness he saw over his many years in combat, which included several decades of reading about all the great battles, imagining he was at each, and a handful of years in World War I and World War II, always near the front, always exposed to danger, as if he was yearning for the glorious death that befell so many other great commanders, securing their legacy for all time.

Again, in awesome guise I rush,
   Stupendous, through the ranks of war,
      Turning to water, with my gaze,
         Hearts that, before, no foe could awe.

The maiden who has strayed from right,
   To me must pay the mead of shame.
      The patriot who betrays his trust,
         To me must owe his tarnished name.

I spare no class, nor cult, nor creed,
   My course is endless through the year.
      I bow all heads and break all hearts,
         All owe me homage—I am FEAR.

THE ATTACK (SEPTEMBER 1916)

Death stalked among the combatants
His scythe with blood was dank;
He reaped, with mirthless energy,
From men of every rank.

From noble and from simple,
The hero and the knave,
His ghastly strokes in shrapnel fell
To fill the common grave.

Now, as the lines draw nearer
The level bullets beat,
From hazing mouths of rifles,
Hid in the yellow wheat.

Youths, who at home were pampered,
Press forward eagerly,
Vying with callow plow boys,
Which first Death's face should see.

While louder and yet louder
Increased the awful roar,
While acrid in their nostrils rose,
The stink of fresh spilled gore.

And now the trench is entered,
The bayonets thrust home;
From mangled flesh, round prodding points,
Ooze out the guts and foam.

They struggle in that rhapsody,
Which only fighters know;
They club and thrust, while trampling,
Torn friend and writhing foe.

Alas! they stagger backward,
Their valorous dash outworn;
They falter, yet an instant,
In the bullet-winnowed corn.

Fear playing on their heartstrings,
In piteous rout they fly;
Save only one, who turns white faced,
Determined there to die.

It is not courage holds him,
But fear in its mightiest form
Born of a race of soldiers,
He dares not face their scorn.

His eyes can see Valhalla
Where, staring from the skies,
The men who fought for England
Watch how their offspring dies.

And then his vision lengthens,
He sees two eyes of blue,
Soft eyes which seem to worship,
Trusting his courage true.

No longer now he falters,
Can man betray such love?
Deserted by his fellows,
His strength comes from above.

He staggers towards the rifles,
He crumples in their flame,
He falls another victim,
But saves a glorious name.

Shame on faint hearts that babble
Of justice and of right,
Yet speak of war as murder
And deride the men who fight.

'Tis only battle raised men
To noblest sacrifice,
And war alone can purge our hearts
Of cowardice and vice.

Speak not of those who perish
As lives wasted in vain;
No more than mother's labour
Has been for naught their pain.

To each of us in peace and war
There comes a time to go;
To each one's friends at such a time
There comes the loss and woe.

But is it not far better
To die one's land to save,
Than having lived in slothful peace
To sink to nameless grave?

Which one of us by peaceful death
Can leave to heirs to come,
The pride which conquers cowardice
To save noble name?

Oh! Glorious god of Battle,
Preserve to us the race,
Of those who scorning worldly gain
Fear death less than disgrace.

Let not our growing affluence
Make us unfit to fight;
But make us eager, now as e'er
To keep our honor bright.

MIGHT-RIGHT (4 NOV. 1916)

When the cave man sat in his stinking lair,
  With his low browed mate hard by;
Gibbering the while he sank his teeth
  In a new killed reindeer's thigh.

Thus he learned that to fight was noble;
  Thus he learned that to shirk was base,
Thus he conquered the creatures one and all,
  And founded a warrior race.

What would he have thought, could his foggy brain,
  Have pictured our hapless day.
When craven souls of dreaming fools
  Should habit our human clay.

When cowards born of Fear and Greed
  Should preach to kindred slaves;
That Right may stand by its self alone,
  And needs not Might to save.

They speak but lies these sexless souls,
  Lies born of fear of strife
And nurtured in soft indulgence
  They see not War is Life.

They dare not admit the truth,
  Though writ in letters red,
That man shall triumph now as then
  By blood, which man has shed.

★ ★ ★

★ ★ ★

No amount of praying could save a soldier who panicked on the battlefield. The Grim Reaper would always snatch up a few unfortunate souls and Lady Luck would gather in the rest of the lucky ones.

On the battlefield, God was but a quiet bystander. Those soldiers who accepted this, who pushed aside their fears, who fought as heroes—even when faced with certain death—belonged to an exclusive club. They were the best of the best of Patton's boys, for they were the ones who had a warrior's soul.

CONQUERING FEAR

There is a time to take counsel of your fears and there is a time to never listen to any fear.

All men are timid on entering any fight. Whether it is the first or the last fight, all of us are timid. Cowards are those who let their timidity get the better of their manhood.

Never stop being ambitious. You have but one life, live it to the fullest of glory and be willing to pay any price.

Do not regard what you do only as "preparation" for doing the same thing more fully or better at some later time. Nothing is ever done twice. There is no next time. This is of special application to war. There is but one time to win a battle or a campaign. It must be won the first time.

Battle is not a terrifying ordeal to be endured. It is a magnificent experience wherein all of the elements that have made man superior to the beasts are present. Courage, self sacrifice, loyalty, help to others, and devotion to duty. As you go in, you will perhaps be a little short of breath, and your knees may tremble. This breathlessness, this tremor, they are not fear. It is simply the excitement which every athlete feels just before the whistle blows. No, you will not fear for you will be borne up and exalted by the proud instinct of our conquering race. You will be inspired by magnificent hate.

Americans play to win at all times. I wouldn't give a hoot in hell for a man who lost and laughed. That's why Americans have never lost nor will ever lose a war.

Cowardice is a disease and it must be checked.

Discipline must be a habit so ingrained that it is stronger than the excitement of battle or the fear of death.

We must remember that victories are not gained solely by selfless devotion. To conquer, we must destroy our enemies. We must not only die gallantly, we must kill devastatingly. The faster and more effectively we kill, the longer we will live to enjoy the priceless fame of conquerors.

Of course, our men are willing to die, but that is not enough. We must be eager to kill, to inflict on the enemy, the hated enemy, all possible wounds, death and destruction. If we die killing, well and good. But, if we fight hard enough, viciously enough, we will kill and live to kill again. We will live to return to our families as conquering heroes.

Each form of specialist, like the aviators, the artillery men, or the tanks, talk as if theirs was the only useful weapon and that if there were enough of them used, the war would soon

Due to the attritions of war, replacements were sent forward to ensure that units maintained their fighting strength. But disproportionately it was these untested combatants who quickly became casualties. General Patton recognized this and called on his battle-hardened veterans to bond with these rookies, for the good of the unit: "War develops a soul in a fighting unit, and where there may not be many of the old men left, it takes very little yeast to leaven a lump of dough. I suppose I might be funny and say it takes very few veterans to leaven a division of doughboys."

The quicker these new combatants acquired the "warrior soul" Patton demanded, the more likely they just might survive to later tell about their experiences in World War II.

end. As a matter of fact, it is the doughboy, in the final analysis, who does the trick.

The true objective of armor is enemy infantry and artillery;
and above all else, his supply installations and command
centers.

It is easy to die for nothing, one should die for something.

Speaking in general, I find that moral courage is the most valuable and usually the most absent characteristic in men. Much of our trouble is directly attributable to the fear of "they."

Men who are apt to die in battle are entitled to what pleasures they can get.

The soldier is the army. No army is better than the soldiers in it. To be a good soldier, a man must have discipline, self-confidence, self-respect, pride in his unit and in his country. He must have a high sense of duty and obligation to his comrades and to his superiors.

To me, it is a never-ending marvel what our soldiers can do.

An amusing incident occurred on this trip. I have always insisted that anti-tank guns be placed where they can see

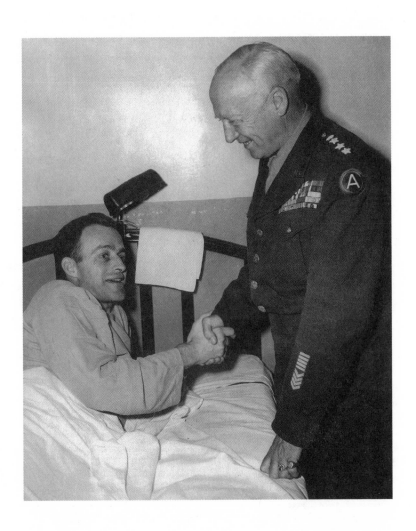

★ ★ ★

During the final weeks of the war in Europe, many Nazi concentration camps were being liberated. When General Patton learned that his son-in-law—Lt. Col. John Waters, captured during the battle for Tunisia—was being held at one of these camps, he ordered a task force from his Third Army to free him. Later at Walter Reed Hospital in Washington, DC, Patton visited Lieutenant Colonel Waters.

without being seen. I came to a crucifix in the middle of a three-way road junction, and sitting exactly under the crucifix was an anti-tank gun completely unconcealed. I gave the NCO in charge the devil for not having carried out my instructions. When I got through he said, "Yes sir, but yesterday we got two tanks from this position." So I had to apologize. Perhaps the sanctity of the location saved the gun?

In peace, the scholar flourishes. In war, the soldier dies. So it comes about that we view our soldiers through the eyes of scholars and attribute to them scholarly virtues.

I'm a hell of a guy. I'm giving the men hell one minute and crying over them the next.

Unless you do your best, the day will come when, tired and hungry, you will halt just short of the goal you were ordered to reach and by halting, you will make useless the efforts and deaths of thousands.

War is a killing business. You must spill the enemy's blood or they will spill yours.

Italy

★ ★ ★

They were young, they were scared, and they all wanted to be somewhere other than where they were, about to go into battle, again. But they knew what had to be done and they knew it required brutality and swiftness. And they knew that fear and hesitation only increased the casualty count.

Death in battle is a function of time. The longer troops remain under fire, the more men get killed. Therefore, everything must be done to speed up movement.

Death, in time, comes to all men. Yes, every man is scared in his first battle. If he says he's not, he's a liar. Some men are cowards but they fight the same as the brave men or they get the hell slammed out of them watching men fight who are just as scared as they are. The real hero is the man who fights even though he is scared. Some men get over their fright in a minute under fire. For some, it takes an hour. For some, it takes days. But a real man will never let his fear of death overpower his honor, his sense of duty to his country and his

innate manhood. Battle is the most magnificent competition in which a human being can indulge. It brings out all that is best and it removes all that is base.

Many American soldiers serving during World War II were of European descent, and their parents or grandparents had come from "the old country." There was some concern that those GIs who were Italian or German might be hesitant to fight against Axis forces, but General Patton didn't feel it was an issue. "They are as good soldiers as anybody else. They are not going to pay any attention and if they are asked to bombard the village of their father or grandfather they are going to bombard it and fight to capture it," he wrote.

Many of you have in your veins German and Italian blood. But remember that these ancestors of yours so loved freedom that they gave up home and country to cross the ocean in search of liberty. The ancestors of the people we shall kill lacked the courage to make such a sacrifice and remained slaves.

My policy of continuous attack is correct. The farther we press, the more stuff we find abandoned that should not be abandoned. The Italians are fighting very well in the face of defeat. They must crack soon.

Back of us stretches a line of men whose acts of valor, of self sacrifice, and of service have been the theme of song and story since long before recorded history began. Our professional ancestors were sung of by the blind poet Homer a thousand years before the Christ. The exploits of which he chanted, and others of like nature, were handed down by word of mouth or in everlasting marble to the time when they might be recorded in writing for the eternal inspiration for the race.

To conquer, we must destroy our enemies. We must not only die gallantly; we must kill devastatingly. The faster and more

effectively you kill, the longer you will live to enjoy the priceless fame of conquerors.

It lurks invisible in that vitalizing spark, intangible, yet as evident as the lightning; the "Warrior Soul."

There was fear in their eyes that was unmistakable. They tried to ignore it, cracked smart-ass jokes, played cards for something to do, but it wouldn't go away, like a black cloud overhead.

Those with battle scars (or who claimed to have them), who'd danced with the devil and lived to fight on, liked to talk about their "heroism" and maybe scare the bejesus out of the new-bies who were about to experience hell on Earth for the first time. Tragically many would not survive to brag about their initiation under fire, their first-time heroic exploits.

"So great were the good-will and devotion of Caesar's soldiers to him, that those who under other generals were in no way superior to ordinary soldiers, were invincible and irresistible and ready to meet any danger for Caesar's glory."

—*Plutarch, writing about Caesar*

War is conflict. Fighting is an elemental exposition of the age-old effort to survive. It is the cold glitter of the attacker's eye that breaks the line, not the point of the bayonet.

As a man who has seen something of war, I am more impressed with the manly virtues it engenders than with the necessary and much exaggerated horrors attendant upon it.

———————————— ★ ★ ★ ————————————

War is brutal and ugly, nothing like the lyricism of poetry. Even the most graphic of war poems still can't capture the sensory overload of actual combat. The persona of George Patton, the Spartan warrior, old blood-and-guts, was a prolific writer of war poems. In "Absolute War," written in August of 1944, he lashed out at the exasperatingly slow way his Allied counterparts waged war, like they were stuck in the mud.

ABSOLUTE WAR

ABSOLUTE WAR (1944)

Now in war we are confronted
with conditions which are strange.
If we accept them we will never win.
Since by being realistic,
as in mundane combats fistic,
We will get a bloody nose and that's a sin.

To avoid such fell disaster,
the result of fighting faster,
We resort to fighting carefully and slow.
We fill up terrestrial spaces
with secure expensive bases
To keep our tax rate high and death rate low.

But with sadness and with sorrow
  we discover to our horror
    That while we build, the enemy gets set.
So despite our fine intentions
  to produce extensive pensions
    We haven't licked the dirty bastard yet.

For in war just as in loving,
  you must always keep on shoving
    Or you'll never get your just reward.

For if you are dilatory in the search
  for lust and glory
    You are up shit creek and
      that's the truth, Oh! Lord.

So let us do real fighting,
    boring in and gouging, biting.
        Let's take a chance
            now that we have the ball.

Let's forget those fine firm bases
    in the dreary shell raked spaces.
        Let's shoot the works and win!
Yes, win it all!

———— ★ ★ ★ ————

He was always immaculately dressed, whether striding with purpose across a smoldering battlefield or riding in his staff car, sitting upright and rigid, "like Washington crossing the Delaware. The General sat looking straight ahead, but undoubtedly loved it. He had a sentimental streak. He wanted his men to admire him as much as he admired himself. And furthermore, God damn it, he wanted to be loved!" recalled author John P. Marquand.

As his soldiers liberated town after town, Patton envisioned previous conquerors journeying down the same roads many centuries previous: "I could almost picture in my mind's eye the small groups of knights and men-at-arms who, by virtue of occupying these strong points, ruled the world as they knew it, and how pitifully weak in numbers and armor they were in comparison with our guns, tanks and infantry, which rolled by them in endless streams."

CHAPTER 18

DESTROYING FORTRESS EUROPE

Through the murk of fact and fable rises to our view this one truth; the history of war is the history of warriors; few in number but mighty in influence. Alexander, not Macedonia, conquered the world. Scipio, not Rome, destroyed Carthage. Marlborough, not the Allies, defeated France. Cromwell, not the Roundheads, dethroned Charles.

Julius Caesar would have a tough time being a Brigadier General in my Army.

The great warriors of history were too busy and often too inept to write contemporaneously of their exploits. What they later put on paper was colored by strivings for enhanced fame or by political conditions then confronting their perished past. The violent simplicity in execution which procured for them

a success and enthralled the world looked pale and unin-
spired on paper, so they invariably seasoned it.

The pacifists are at it again. I met a "visiting fireman" of great
eminence who told me that this was to be the "last war." I
told him that such statements since 2600 B.C. had signed
the death warrants of millions of young men. He replied with
the stock lie, "Oh yes, but things are different now." My God!
Will they never learn?

*Before going into battle, General Patton believed in studying his opponent for strengths and
weaknesses, tendencies and vulnerabilities. He also read the historical record of previous campaigns in the same region. For the push across France, he lugged along the six-volume set of the*
History of the Norman Conquest, *by British historian Edward Freeman.*

*Later, in the push across northern Europe, Patton also read a book written by the one
enemy commander many considered his equal—Erwin Rommel, who wrote* Infantry
Attacks, *which revealed the field marshal's combat experiences in World War I.*

The last stand was made in the mountains southwest of Palermo, which was a most difficult nut to crack, but was finally done with artillery fire and tanks. As we approached, the hills on each side were burning. We then started down a long road cut out of the side of a cliff which went through an almost continuous village. The street was full of people shouting, "Down with Mussolini!" and "Long Live America." When we got into the town, the same thing went on. Those who arrived before dark had flowers thrown on the road in front of them . . .

I'm proud to fight here beside you. Now let's cut the guts out of those Krauts and get the Hell to Berlin.

I saw a lot of dead Germans yesterday frozen in funny attitudes. I got some good pictures, but did not have my color camera, which was a pity, as they were a pale claret color.

★ ★ ★

I don't want to get any messages saying that, "We are holding our position." We're not holding anything! Let the Hun do that. We are advancing constantly and we're not interested in holding on to anything except the enemy. We're going to hold on to him by the nose and we're going to kick him in

the ass; we're going to go through him like crap through a
goose.

There can never be too many projectiles in a battle. Whether
they are thrown by cannon, rockets, or recoilless devices is
immaterial. The purpose of all these instruments is identical
. . . namely, is deluge the enemy with fire.

Infantry must move forward to close with the enemy. It must
shoot in order to move . . . To halt under fire is folly. To halt
under fire and not fire back is suicide. Officers must set the
example.

It is only by doing things others have not that one can
advance.

Courage is fear holding on a minute longer.

One of the chief defects of an airborne division is the fact
that it never has anything it needs after it lands. No tanks, no
adequate artillery, and no transportation.

After nearly two years of being accustomed to the inarticulate shapes of the Arab women, the over-stuffed profiles of the Italians, and to the boyish figures of the British women, the obtrusive and meticulously displayed figures of the Norman and Brittan women is quite striking. In a way they remind me of a British engine with two bumpers in front and powerful driving wheels behind.

When any group of soldiers is under small arms fire, it is evident that the enemy can see them; therefore, men should be able to see the enemy but seldom are. When this situation arises, they must fire at the portions of the hostile terrain which probably conceals enemy small arms weapons. I know for a fact that such procedure invariably produces an effect and generally stops hostile fire. Always remember that it is much better to waste ammunition than lives. It takes at least eighteen years to produce a soldier and only a few months to produce ammunition.

★ ★ ★

From Palermo and Rome, to Paris and Luxembourg, liberated villagers were overjoyed as Allied forces routed their Nazi occupiers. General Patton was the conquering hero who led his troops in battle and sometimes at the head of the victory parade, but often he watched the festivities from a distance, already preparing for the next confrontation, the next skirmish with the fleeing Nazis.

★ ★ ★

Americans love to fight. All real Americans love the sting of battle.

★ ★ ★

No commander drove his troops harder than George S. Patton, but no leader cared more for them either. And while many senior officers made their tactical decisions far from the front lines, a safe distance from danger, Patton prowled the combat zone regularly. He felt it was the best way to assess the rapid movements in war, and redirect the offensive as needed.

"[T]here was no leader in whom the soldiers placed more confidence or under whom they showed more daring. He was fearless in exposing himself to danger and perfectly self-possessed in the presence of danger. He was by far the foremost both of the cavalry and the infantry, the first to enter the fight and the last to leave the field," wrote Titus Livius on Hannibal, but he could have easily been writing many years later about George Patton.

The psychology of the fighting man is a strange thing. Early, well before dawn, I watched men of an almost green division, who were soaking wet and cold, cross a swollen river in the face of steep hills which were packed with concrete gun emplacements, machine guns, mines, and barbed wire. They crossed without hesitation and they walked right through that concentration of fire. They never hesitated once. Later in the day, I came across another outfit which was stalled along an open road. Do you know what was holding them back? It was a length of yellow string which was tied across their path between trees. No one in the outfit dared to touch it.

I guess that it is the unknown which a man faces that he is scared of.

Put your heart and soul into being expert killers with your weapons.

The soldier is the Army. No Army is better than its soldiers.

Wars may be fought with weapons, but they are won by men. It is the spirit of the men who follow and the man who leads that gains the victory.

All men are afraid in battle. The coward is the one who lets his fear overcome his sense of duty.

Our men are really grim fighters. I would hate to be the enemy.

★ ★ ★

Each man must not think only of himself, but also of his buddy fighting beside him. We don't want yellow cowards in this Army. They should be killed off like rats. If not, they will go home after this war and breed more cowards. The brave men will breed more brave men. Kill off the Goddamned cowards and we will have a nation of brave men.

One of the bravest men that I ever saw was a fellow on top of a telegraph pole in the midst of a furious firefight in Tunisia. I stopped and asked what the hell he was doing up there at a time like that. He answered, "Fixing the wire, Sir." I asked, "Isn't that a little unhealthy right about now?" He answered, "Yes Sir, but the Goddamned wire has to be fixed." I asked, "Don't those planes strafing the road bother you?" And he answered, "No, Sir, but you sure as hell do!"

Now, there was a real man. A real soldier. There was a man who devoted all he had to his duty, no matter how seemingly insignificant his duty might appear at the time, no matter how great the odds.

As he directed his troops across France and northern Europe, George Patton knew he was traversing territory that had been conquered by the Romans and the Huns, Charles and Napoleon and Black Jack Pershing. He studied the past conquests to assure his own victories in 1944 and 1945.

In many instances, Patton told others he had been at battles that had occurred in centuries gone, hinting that maybe he believed in reincarnation: After the 94th Division took over Saarburg in Germany, in late February of 1945, Patton recalled that the former king of Bohemia, John the Blind, had occupied the castle there. He died in 1346 during the war between the French and the English. Patton would later say to his daughter, "I was there" to witness the demise of John the Blind.

You must never halt because some other unit is stuck. If you push on, you will relieve the pressure on the adjacent unit and it will accompany you.

I also re-read the "Norman Conquest" by Freeman, paying particular attention to the roads used by William the Conqueror during his operations in Normandy and Brittany. The roads used in those days had to be on ground which was always practical.

We have got by due to persistence and on the ability to make plans fit circumstances. The other armies try to make circumstances fit plans.

Without benefit of aerial bombardment, ground smoke, artillery preparation and airborne assistance, the Third Army at 2200 hours, Thursday, 22nd March, 1945, crossed the Rhine River.

The enemy is as ignorant of the situation as are we.

Dear SHAEF, I have just pissed into the Rhine River. For God's sake, send some gasoline.

If I could only steal some gasoline, I could win this war.

One sentinel, reinforced, stopped 17 Germans in American uniforms. 15 were shot, 2 died suddenly.

Now there is nothing to stop me. We have fresh divisions arriving. We've mastered the air. We have, after some tough lessons, the best weapons in the world. We can march into Berlin, Vienna, Prague, and Belgrade with people throwing flowers in our path. But, from Washington or London or somewhere they'll stop us. Otherwise, it might offend the Goddamned Russians. Before that happens, I'm hoping to get out of here to fight the Japs. If not, I'm going to resign and tell the people in my country what is the truth.

★ ★ ★

Europe is crisscrossed by rivers, which served as natural boundaries, allowing Nazi forces to reinforce defensive positions along key vantage points and prevent the Allies from successfully crossing over. Whether by utilizing the few remaining bridges still intact or piling into fragile assault boats, the troops had to get to the other side to continue the push deep into Fortress Europe.

We promised the Europeans freedom. It would be worse than dishonorable not to see they have it. This might mean war with the Russians, but what of it? They have no Air Force anymore, their gasoline and ammunition supplies are low. I've seen their miserable supply trains; mostly wagons drawn by beaten up old horses or oxen. I'll say this; the Third Army alone with very little help and with damned few casualties, could lick what is left of the Russians in six weeks. You mark my words. Don't ever forget them. Someday we will have to fight them and it will take six years and cost us six million lives.

You are not beaten until you admit it.

In battle, the soldier enters a lottery with death as the stake. The only saving clauses in this gamble lie in time and the demoralizing effect produced on the enemy by the rapid and uninterrupted advance of the attacker.

Americans do not surrender.

★ ★ ★

I drove . . . through the forest which we had attacked so
heavily with artillery during the Bastogne operation. The
effect of the use of proximity fuse on the forest was very
remarkable.

You could see the exact angle of impact of all the projectiles, which had burst about 30 feet above the highest tree-
tops. After bursting, they cut the trees at an angle of about
40 degrees down near the ground. However, it seemed to me
then . . . that, in heavy woods, the proximity fuse is not efficient, as the timber absorbs the fragments.

★ ★ ★

*When American forces were halted near Nancy, in France, Nazi forces surrounded them and
ordered them to surrender. But the Battling Bastards of Bastogne refused, hunkering down to
wait for reinforcements. In one of his most brilliant battle tactics, General Patton ordered some
of his units to disengage from the fight, wheel around and head to Bastogne, busting through
the German lines and driving them off.*

★ ★ ★

With the dismantling of Hitler's Thousand Year Reich, hundreds of towns and villages were destroyed, leaving their residents homeless and destitute, scavenging for food, seeking shelter wherever they could find it, and searching for loved ones lost in the chaos of war.

For such woods the delayed action fuse, which bursts only on hitting heavy trees close to the ground, is preferable.

One continues to learn about war by practicing war.

. . . at Saarlautern, I crossed the bridge over the river under alleged fire. It was purely a motion on my part to show the soldiers that generals could get shot at. I was not shot at very much.

The crossing of the three divisions of these rivers [the Our and Sauer Rivers] was a magnificent feat of arms. The rivers were in flood to such an extent that the barbed wire along the Siegfried Line, which abutted on the rivers, was under water, and, when the men disembarked from the boats, they were caught in it. The whole hillside was covered with German pillboxes and barbed wire. A civilian observer told me afterward that he did not see how human beings could be brave enough to succeed in such an attack.

. . . the 10th Armored Division was in Trier and had captured a bridge over the Moselle intact. The capture of this bridge was due to the heroic act of Lieutenant Colonel J.J. Richardson, deceased. He was riding in the leading vehicle of his battalion of armored infantry when he saw the wires leading to the demolition charges at the far end of the bridge.

* * *

In March of 1945, Patton's Third Army "bounced the Rhine," the final obstacle as Allied forces pushed into the Fatherland. He ordered them to get across as quickly as possible, knowing how perilous river crossing could be, with troops vulnerable to enemy gunners. "No one realizes the terrible value of the 'unforgiving minute' except me. Someway I will get on yet," he wrote in his journal in late August of 1944.

As he was crossing over on a pontoon bridge, Patton stopped to spit in the Rhine. (Some accounts stated he took the opportunity to relieve himself.) Then, as he got to the other side, he deliberately stumbled, reenacting what William the Conqueror and Scipio Africanus had done many years previous, when they too tripped, grabbed a handful of soil, and declared the conquered territories as their own.

Jumping out of the vehicle, he raced across the bridge under heavy fire and cut the wires.

The acid test of battle brings out the pure metal.

I just took Trier with only two divisions. Do you want me to give it back?

The Third Army starts attacking in the morning, but we will go slow so the others can catch up.

Throughout history wars have been lost because of armies not crossing rivers.

The 21st Army Group was supposed to cross the Rhine River on 24th March, 1945, and in order to be ready for this "earthshaking" event, Mr. Churchill wrote a speech congratulating Field Marshall Montgomery on the "first" assault crossing over the Rhine River in modern history. This speech was recorded and through some error on the part of the British Broadcasting Corporation, was broadcast. In spite of the fact that the Third Army had been across the Rhine River for some THIRTY-SIX HOURS.

The Prayer . . . to Halt the Rain

During the intensity of sustained combat, Patton hated delays of any type, including inclement weather. In December of 1944, his forces were stalled in northern Europe, due to continuous rains and he wanted them stopped by any means possible. His meteorologists could do nothing to quell his frustrations, so then Patton called on the Third Army chaplain, Col. T. H. O'Neill, to do what he could. The chaplain wasn't exactly sure what Patton expected of him. Patton wanted him to write a prayer, to halt the rain.

"May I say, General, that it usually isn't a customary thing among men of my profession to pray for clear weather, to kill fellow men."

Patton didn't give a damn what was "customary." He knew exactly what he wanted, and if the chaplain couldn't follow orders, Patton would find someone who would. Colonel O'Neill fought with his conscience, then reluctantly wrote "The Prayer to Halt the Rain." Patton had it printed on the back of Christmas greetings, and distributed to the troops, two days before Christmas.

Patton did read the Bible regularly, but there was some debate as to whether or not he actually believed in Divine Intervention . . . or if he had any influence with the Good Lord. What is not in question is the simple fact that on Christmas Day of 1944, the rains stopped, and the Third Army immediately got back to what they did best, and that was to kill Krauts!

Patton wrote in his journal: "Christmas dawned clear and cold, lovely weather for killing Germans, although the thought seemed somewhat at variance with the spirit of the day."

THE PRAYER TO HALT THE RAIN
. . . AND RESUME THE KILLING!

Almighty and most merciful Father,
we humbly beseech Thee,
or Thy great goodness,
to restrain these immoderate rains
with which we have had to contend.

Grant us fair weather for Battle.

Graciously hearken to us as soldiers
who call upon Thee that,
armed with Thy power,
we may advance from victory to victory,
and crush the oppression and wickedness
of our enemies, and establish Thy justice
among men and nations. Amen.

---------------------- ★ ★ ★ ----------------------

The United States and Russia were Allies in defeating Nazi Germany, and everyone smiled
for the cameras when they linked up at the Elbe River in the final weeks of the war. George
Patton's juggernaut known as the Third Army was clearly the more potent force but they were
ordered to halt the advance, so Russian forces could capture Berlin, thus ending the Thousand
Year Reich.

Patton, who was aware that Josef Stalin was just as much a ruthless dictator as Adolf Hit-
ler, wanted to attack Berlin and kill "that Nazi bastard," then keep right on going, all the way
to Moscow and rid the world of Stalin too.

Tin soldier politicians in Washington have allowed us to kick the Hell out of one bastard and at the same time forced us to help establish a second one as evil or more evil than the first . . . This time we'll need almighty God's constant help if we're to live in the same world with Stalin and his murdering cutthroats.

Peace is going to be a hell of a letdown.

The world has no use for a defeated soldier and nothing too good for a victor.

Someone must win the war and also the peace.

Perpetual peace is a futile dream.

Let's keep our boots polished, bayonets sharpened, and present a picture of force and strength to the Russians. This is the only language that they understand and respect. If you fail to do this, then I would like to say that we have had a victory over the Germans, and have disarmed them, but we have lost the war.

With the defeat of Nazi Germany, George Patton was ready to head on to Moscow and defeat Stalin and the Red Army.

Instead, Patton returned to a hero's welcome in Boston, in June of 1945, decked out in all his finery. After another ovation in Los Angeles, he returned to Germany to become military governor of Bavaria.

When the American Expeditionary Force entered the Great War, George Patton was an Army captain. He observed French Renault tanks lumbering across battlefields littered with barbed wire, trenches, and fortifications. He was the only American officer who foresaw the potential of an armored force. Two decades later he was a general, America's biggest proponent of tank warfare.

The following poem, written at the end of World War I, still had relevance in the mid-1940s, as Hitler's Thousand Year Reich was destroyed:

PEACE (NOVEMBER 11, 1918)

I stood in the flag-decked cheering crowd
   Where all but I were gay
     And gazing on their extecy (as spelled)
      My heart shrank in dismay.

For theirs was the joy of the "little folk"
   The cruel glee of the weak
     Who, banded together, have slain the strong
      Which none alone dared seak. (as spelled)

The Boche we know was a hideous beast
   Beyond our era's ban
     But soldiers still must honor the Hun
      As a mighty fighting man.

The vice he had was strong and real
    Of virtue he had none.
        Yet he fought the world remorselessly
        And very nearly won . . .

While the conquerors here—this cheering mob
    With obscene mind and soul
        Who look but on peace as a means to glut—
        Their life's one sensuous goal.

And looking forward I could see
    Like a festering sewer
        Full of the fecal Pacifists
        Which peace makes us endure.

I saw around the placid hearths of homes
    Sleek virtues soft and cheap
        Which neither make the soul to soar
        Nor cause the heart to leap.

Those bootless, cramping, little lusts
    The vices mean and small
        Vile scurrying of avarice
        Weak lusts by fear held thrall.

None of the hold and blatant sin
    The disregard of pain,
        The glorious deeds of sacrifice
        Which follow in wars train.

Instead of these the little lives
  Will blossom as before,
    Pale bloom of creatures all too weak
    To hear the light of war.

While we whose spirits wider range
  Can grasp the joys of strife
    Will moulder in the virtuous vice
    Of futile peaceful life.

We can but hope that e're we drown
  'Neath treacle floods of grace
    The tuneless horns of mighty Mars
    Once more shall rouse the Race.

When such times come, Oh! God of War
  Great that we pass midst strife
    Knowing once more the white hot joy
    Of taking human life.

Then pass in peace, blood-glutted Boche
  And when we too shall fall
    We'll clasp our gory hands as friends
    In high Valhallas's Hall.

In 1919, during the final days of The Great War, Patton wrote to his wife about an incident when some of his men encountered a German gun emplacement: "One of my tanks was attacking a machine gun when the gun in the tank jammed so the men decided to run down the machine gun. The two (Germans) fired to the last and the tank went over them. Next day they were found still holding their gun, though dead. There could be nothing finer in war. My men buried them and put up crosses." In battle Patton would destroy his enemies. In death, he knew they deserved a final tribute . . . "Salute the Brave."

MOURNING THE DEAD

A SOLDIER'S BURIAL
(1919, PUBLISHED IN 1943)

Not midst the chanting of the Requiem Hymn,
Nor with the solemn ritual of prayer,
'Neath misty shadows from the oriel glass,
and dreamy perfume of the incensed air
Was he interred;

But in the subtle stillness after fight,
and the half light between the night and the day,
We dragged his body
all besmeared with mud,
and dropped it, clod-like,
back into the clay.

Yet who shall say that he was not content,
   Or missed the prayers,
      or drone of chanting choir,
   He who had heard all day the Battle Hymn
      Sung on all sides
         by a thousand throats of fire.

What painted glass can lovelier shadows cast
   Than those the evening skies shall ever shed,
      While, mingled with their light,
         Red Battle's Sun
      Completes in magic colors o'er our dead
         The flag for which they died.

FINAL THOUGHTS

There is one great thing that you men will all be able to say after this war is over and you are home once again. You may be thankful that twenty years from now when you are sitting by the fireplace with your grandson on your knee and he asks you what you did in the great World War II, you WON'T have to cough, shift him to the other knee and say, "Well, your Granddaddy shoveled shit in Louisiana."

No, Sir, you can look him straight in the eye and say, "Son, your Granddaddy rode with the Great Third Army and a Son-of-a-Goddamned-Bitch named Georgie Patton!"

VALOR
(IN LETTER FROM PATTON TO HIS DAD, IN 1945)

When all hearts are opened,
and all the secrets known,
When guile and lies are banished,
and subterfuge is gone.

When God rolls up the curtain,
and hidden truths appear,
When the ghastly light of Judgment Day,
Brings past and present near . . .

Then shall we know what once we knew,
Before wealth dimmed our sight,
That of all sins, the blackest is
The pride which will not fight.

The meek and pious have a place,
and necessary are,
But valor pales their puny rays,
As does the sun a star.

What race of men since time began,
Has ever yet remained,
Who trusted not its own right hand,
Or from brave deeds refrained?

Yet spite the fact for ages known,
and by all lands displayed,
We still have those who prate of peace,
and say that war is dead.

Yes vandals rise who seek to snatch
The laurels from the brave,
and dare defame heroic dead,
Now filling hero graves.

They speak of those who love,
Like Christ's, exceeds the lust of life
and murderers slain to no avail,
A useless sacrifice.

With infamy without a name,
They mock our fighting youth,
and dare decry great hearts who die,
Battling for right and truth.

Woe to the land which, heeding them,
Lets avarice gain the day,
and trusting gold it's right to hold,
Lets manly might decay.

Let us, while willing yet for peace,
Still keep our valor high,
So when our time of battle comes,
We shall not fear to die.

Make love of life and ease be less,
Make love of country more.
So shall our patriotism be
More than an empty roar.

Cold, callous, brutal, insensitive, vindictive . . .

Over the course of his military service, those terms were just some of the harsher ones others used to describe George Patton. Maybe he did have a crusty exterior, but he also had a soft spot that few saw or knew of.

During a conversation with Henry J. Taylor from the Scripps-Howard newspapers in mid-March of 1945, on the eve of the assault on the Rhine River, Patton told him: "Who do you suppose knows what it means to order an attack and know that in a few hours thousands of our boys are going to be killed or hurt? War is my work and I know I sound sometimes as though I liked it; perhaps I do, but this war hurts everybody and at times like this I wish I could just fight single-handed, alone."

On Armistice Day of 1945, Patton visited the military cemetery in Palermo, Sicily, paying tribute to those who fell in battle there.

For death is nothing, comfort less,
Valor is all in all;
Base nations who depart from it,
Shall sure and justly fall.

IN MEMORIAM (1918)

The war is over
and we pass to pleasure after pain
Except those few who ne'er shall see
their native land again.
To one of these my memory turns
noblest of the noble slain
To Captain English of the Tanks,
who never shall return.

Yet should some future war
exact of me the final debt
My fondest hope would be to tread
the path which he has set.
For faithful unto God and man
and to his country true
He died to live forever
in the hearts of those he knew.

Patton wanted nothing more than to die in battle, violently, valiantly, heroically. Instead, after returning from a day of pheasant hunting in Bavaria, General Patton was involved in a minor traffic accident, on the 9th of December in 1945. Though there was little damage to his staff car, Patton had sustained a broken neck and was paralyzed. He held on for twelve days but finally gave up the fight on the 21st. He was buried at the military cemetery at Hamm in Luxembourg, alongside several thousand of his Third Army soldiers. The greatest battlefield commander of World War II's European Campaign had rejoined his boys, his valiant heroes.

May all their ever-afters be peaceful ones.

PHOTO CAPTIONS
AND SOURCES

Page xi: Cadet George Patton. Courtesy of the Patton Museum.

Page xiii: In the presence of his troops, Patton consistently displayed a "tough as nails" image. Courtesy of the Patton Museum.

Page xiv: Major General Patton. US Army.

Page xxi: Saying goodbye to Dad, who'll be shipping out "for the duration." National Archives.

Page 11: US 23rd Infantry soldiers during World War I's battle of St. Mihiel. National Archives.

Page 12: Col. George Patton in front of a French tank in World War I. US Army Signal Corps.

Page 18: American tanks in England in early 1944. National Archives.

Page 21: 36th Infantry Regiment GIs on M4 Sherman tank. US Army.

Page 22: Soldiers watch an aerial dogfight between Allied and Nazi planes. US Army Signal Corps.

Page 24: Easter Service in 1945 for American soldiers. US Army.

Page 26: XX Corps tank with infantry soldiers in France. US Army.

Page 29: Infantry hop on board anything heading to the front. US Army.

Page 30: Artillery firing at Carenten, France, 1944. US Army Signal Corps.

Page 34: While visiting the Spanish Riding Academy, Patton—himself an accomplished equestrian—tested a gallant steed, and showed off his own prowess. US Army Signal Corps.

Page 36: First Army soldiers approach a French village in 1944. US Army.

Page 39: Algiers illuminated by antiaircraft fire and searchlights during a German air raid. US Army.

Page 40: During the Allied invasion of North Africa, transport planes carried Army paratroopers, while infantry forces converged via naval task force. US Army Air Corps.

Page 42: US troops launch a Bailey Bridge across a river. US Army Signal Corps.

Page 44: Hand to hand combat at basic training. US Army.

Page 46: Bayonet drills at basic training. US Army Photo.

Page 48: Navy and Marine Corps recruits at boot camp acquired the same toughness required of Army trainees. US Navy.

Page 52: An artillery crew with the US II Corps fires on Nazi units near El Guettar, Tunisia, in March of 1943. US Army Military History Institute.

Page 53: Two 101st Airborne soldiers at Bastogne. Imperial War Museum.

Page 56: Patton watching troop movements during the Louisiana Maneuvers, September 1941. National Archives.

Page 58: Patton believed tanks supported the infantry, not just by providing protection but also heavy firepower. US Army.

Page 61: PFC Thomas Gilgore of the 8th Infantry Division during a lull in fighting near the Huertgen Forest. US Army.

Page 65: Villagers in Dambach, Germany buried an American soldier killed there. His grave is checked by another soldier. National Archives.

Page 66: Evacuating the wounded at Monte Belvedere. US Army.

Page 68: Some were critically wounded, barely clinging to life; others would be patched up and thrown back into battle. National Archives.

Page 70: Medal of Honor recipient Audie Murphy. US Army.

Page 73: An Army medic cares for a wounded soldier and preps him for evacuation to a field hospital. US Army.

Page 76: Military religious service at London's Coventry, bombed out due to Nazi V-bombs. Imperial War Museum.

Page 78: An American soldier in the invasion of North Africa in November of 1942. Imperial War Museum.

Page 79: Major General Patton reads a compass while standing beside an M3 Stuart tank, at the Desert Training Center in California. Courtesy of Patton Museum.

Page 82: 9th Armored Division forces rush to Bastogne to relieve American soldiers trapped there by the German Wehrmacht. US Army.

Page 83: Paratroopers of the 101st Airborne Division near St. Marcouf in France display captured Nazi flag. US Army.

Page 84: A deadly arsenal of shells was carefully stowed before going into battle. US Army.

Page 87: An American tank offloads from a transport ship at Anzio in May 1944. US Army.

Page 88: Soldiers of the 370th Infantry Regiment approach Prato, Italy in April 1945. US Army.

Page 89: GIs climbing over beach breakfront. US Army.

Page 90: A Sherman tank from the 1st Armored Division enters Rosswalden, Germany in April 1945. National Archives.

Page 92: GIs pose in front of wrecked German tank with Swastika flag. National Archives.

Page 95: GIs wait for the enemy to attack. *YANK* Magazine.

Page 96: Portrait of Erwin Rommel, the Desert Fox. Bundesarchiv Painting, courtesy of the Patton Museum.

Page 98: Nazi soldier with his children in Brussels, in 1944. Imperial War Museum.

Page 99: A German soldier briefs members of the Hitler Youth defending Berlin in February 1945. Library of Congress.

Page 100: Adolf Hitler at Nazi Party rally in Nuremberg. Library of Congress.

Page 101: Adolf Hitler raises his arm and every member of Nazi Germany's Reichstag responds with "Sieg Heil." National Archives.

Page 102: Flemish recruits train to serve with Nazi forces. Bundesarchiv.

Page 103: At the base of the cliffs at Normandy, the wounded wait to be evacuated, June 1944. US Army Signal Corps.

Page 104: Reich's Air Marshal Hermann Goring inspects the troops during a military ceremony. Imperial War Museum.

Page 105: Captured Nazi officer eating C-rations in the rubble of Saarbrucken near the end of the war. National Archives.

Page 106: A Nazi machine-gun crew during training prior to being sent into combat. Bundesarchiv.

Page 107: Adolf Hitler at Nazi Party rally in 1936 in Nuremberg. US Army.

Page 108: Japanese soldiers celebrate an early victory in the Pacific Campaign, but it wasn't long before they would suffer a string of devastating defeats. National Archives.

Page 109: Army private Forrest Darr shows off his souvenir Nazi medals to his buddy Corp. Marvin Wells, both of the 104th Infantry Division during the Rhineland Campaign. US Army Signal Corps.

Page 112: A chaplain holds mass on Mount Suribachi, Iwo Jima. US Navy.

Page 113: Army private Chester Kolano from Buffalo kneels at the grave of one of his buddies. National Archives.

Page 114: Patton talks with one of his commanders at Messina. US Army.

Page 116: GIs on a transport ship bound for Normandy, France. US Coast Guard.

Page 119: Gen. Dwight D. Eisenhower. US Army.

Page 122: General Patton and General Eisenhower. US Army.

Page 123: Gen. George Patton and Gen. Omar Bradley. Courtesy of the Patton Museum.

Page 126: The American commanders—Bradley, Eisenhower, and Patton—among the rubble at Bastogne. US Army.

Page 131: General Patton on his landing barge bound for the beach at Fedala, Sicily. National Archives.

Page 133: Three Allied commanders: Omar Bradley, George Patton, and Bernard Montgomery, who sometimes battled each other while defeating the Nazis. Imperial War Museum.

Page 135: The Sherman tank, which first appeared at El Alamein in 1942, was used by all of the Allied forces. US Army.

Page 137: General Patton gives guidance to his field commanders in Sicily. US Army.

Page 139: Patton, his faithful pit bull—Willie—and his Third Army commanders. US Army.

Page 142: Three Seventh Army soldiers look down on a French village during a mortar and artillery barrage. US Army.

Page 143: GIs crossing the Rhine at Oberwesel, Germany in March 1945. US Army Signal Corps.

Page 144: Soldiers from the US Medical Corps carry the wounded from Vaux, France in July of 1918. National Archives.

Page 150: GIs on transport ship wait to go ashore at Oran, North Africa. National Archives.

Page 153: A deadly combination: armor supported by infantry. National Archives.

Page 154: A wary GI watches for enemy snipers. *YANK* Magazine.

Page 155: Eyes open, head on a swivel, fire before fired on, remain on the move, and just maybe they'll get through it alive and in one piece. US Army.

Page 157: During the battle for Tunisia, Lt. Col. John Waters was captured, and detained in a German concentration camp, which was later liberated by Patton's Third Army. Patton later visited with Lieutenant

Colonel Waters while he was recuperating at Walter Reed Hospital in Washington, DC. National Archives.

Page 159: Combat-hardened soldiers in Italy. *YANK* Magazine.

Page 160: American tanks maneuver down a narrow trail in the Huertgen Forest during the Battle of the Bulge. National Archives.

Page 161: Soldiers cautiously enter the Italian village of Caiazzo. US Army.

Page 163: GIs on transport ship headed for Tunisia. National Archives.

Page 164: Troops on board a landing craft bound for Normandy's Utah Beach. National Archives.

Page 166: Tanks from the US Ninth Army push deep into Fortress Europe. Imperial War Museum.

Page 168: 135th Infantry Division soldiers man a machine gun in the snow, at Bastogne. US Army Signal Corps.

Page 170: Fifth Army tanks enter Rome. US Army.

Page 172: By the end of 1944, American soldiers thought they might be home by Christmas. Then the Nazis launched a last-ditch offensive, known as the Battle of the Bulge, in the Huertgen Forest. US Army.

Page 175: While training in England, American paratroopers prepare for a practice jump, in October 1942. US Army.

Page 176: Allied troops march in liberated Paris. US Army.

Page 177: Soldiers of the 5th Infantry Division in fortress city of Metz. Imperial War Museum.

Page 180: Major General Patton in front of tank during stateside war maneuvers. US Army Signal Corps.

Page 182: Massed American tanks rumble across the North African flatlands. US Army.

Page 183: A GI looks down on the bridge at Remagen, which spanned the Rhine River. National Archives.

Page 185: After Nazi forces surrounded American troops at Bastogne, armor and infantry units were rushed in to drive back the Germans. US Army.

Page 186: Their home destroyed, this mother and her three children search for food, shelter, family, and friends. National Archives.

Page 188: Four-Star General Patton. US Army.

Page 189: Soldiers of the Seventh Army cross the Danube River. US Army.

Page 192: American and Russian soldiers celebrate near Torgau, Germany. National Archives.

Page 194: In the final weeks of the war, German army units surrendered en masse to American forces. National Archives.

Page 198: An elderly German woman returns to what's left of her home at the end of the war. US Army Signal Corps.

Page 202: A lone GI in a northern European forest. US Army.

Page 205: On November 11, 1945—Armistice Day—General Patton visited the military cemetery at Palermo, Sicily. Courtesy of the Patton Museum.

Page 207: A temporary grave is marked with a simple cross and a helmet. US Army.

BIBLIOGRAPHY

Allen, Col. Robert S. *Lucky Forward*. New York: The Vanguard Press, 1947.

Army Times. Warrior: The Story of General George S. Patton. New York: GP Putnam's Sons, 1967.

Ayer, Frederick. *Before the Colors Fade: Portrait of a Soldier. George S. Patton*. Boston: Houghton Mifflin, 1964.

Blumenson, Martin. *The Patton Papers*. Boston: Houghton Mifflin, 1974.

———. "George S. Patton: Extraordinary Leader; Extraordinary Man." John Biggs Cincinnati Lectures in Military Leadership and Command. Virginia Military Institute Foundation, Lexington, VA, 1987.

———. "The Many Faces of George S. Patton, Jr." Speech at the US Air Force Academy, Colorado Springs, CO, 1972.

D'Este, Carlo. *Patton: A Genius for War*. New York: Harper Collins Publishers, 1995.

Devaney, John. *Blood and Guts*. New York: Julian Messner, 1982.

Dietrich, Steve E. "The Professional Reading of General George S. Patton Jr." *Journal of Military History*, October 1989.

Essame, H. *Patton—A Study in Command*. New York: Charles Scribner's Sons, 1974.

Farago, Ladislas. *Patton: Ordeal and Triumph*. New York: Ivan Obolensky, 1963.

———. *The Last Days of Patton*. New York: McGraw Hill, 1980.

Finke, Blythe Foote. *General Patton: Fearless Military Leader*. Charlotteville, NY: SamHar Press, 1972.

Frankel, Nat, and Larry Smith. *Patton's Best*. New York: Hawthorn Books, 1978.

Hackworth, David H. "Bring Back Blood and Guts Patton." *Parameters*, September 1987.

Hatch, Alden. *George Patton: General in Spurs*. New York: Julian Messner, 1950.

Hirshson, Stanley P. *General Patton: A Soldier's Life*. New York: HarperCollins, 2002.

Hogg, Ian V. *The Biography of General George S. Patton*. New York: Gallery Books, 1982.

Hymel, Kevin M. *Patton's Photographs: War As He Saw It*. Dulles, VA: Potomac Books, 2010.

Irving, David. *The War Between the Generals*. New York: Congdon and Lattes, 1981.

Mellor, William. *Patton, Fighting Man*. New York: Putnam, 1946.

Nye, Roger H. *The Patton Mind: The Professional Development of an Extraordinary Leader*. Garden City, NY: Avery Publishing Group, 1993.

Patton, George S., Jr. *War As I Knew It*. Boston: Houghton Mifflin, 1947.

———. "Success in War." *Cavalry Journal*, January 1931.

George S. Patton Jr. Papers, archived in the Manuscript Division of the Library of Congress.

George S. Patton Jr. Papers, archived at the US Army Military History Institute, Carlisle Barracks in Carlisle, PA.

George S. Patton Jr. Papers, archived in the Special Collections of the US Military Academy at West Point, NY.

George S. Patton Jr. Papers, archived at the Henry E. Huntington Library at San Marino, CA.

Pearl, Jack. *Blood and Guts Patton: The Swashbuckling Life Story of America's Most Daring and Controversial General.* Derby, CO: Monarch, 1961.

Pfannes, Charles E. and Victor A. Salamone. *The Great Commanders of World War II: The Americans.* New York: Zebra Books, 1981.

Polk, James H. "Patton: 'You Might As Well Die a Hero.'" *Army* magazine, December 1975.

Prioli, Carmine, ed. *Lines of Fire: The Poems of General George S. Patton Jr.* Lewiston, NY: Edwin Mellen Press, 1991.

Province, Charles M. *The Patton Principles.* San Diego, CA: CMP Productions, 1978.

———. *Patton's One Minute Messages: Tactical Leadership Skills for Business Managers.* Novato, CA: Presidio Press, 1995.

Robichon, Jacques. *The Second D-Day.* New York: Walker and Company, 1962.

Rodgers, Russ. *Historic Photos of General George Patton.* Nashville: Turner Publishing, 2007.

Semmes, Harry, *Portrait of Patton.* New York: Paperback Library, 1955.

US Military Academy Archives at West Point.

Weigley, Russell. *Eisenhower's Lieutenants.* Bloomington: Indiana University Press, 1981.

Whiting, Charles. *Patton.* New York: Ballantine Books, 1970.

ABOUT THE AUTHOR

Gary Bloomfield was Army Journalist of the Year in 1976, Managing Editor for *VFW* magazine, and Senior Editor for *Faces of Victory Europe* and *Faces of Victory Pacific*. He is the author of *Maxims of General Patton*; *I Will Be an American Someday Soon*; and *Duty, Honor, Victory: America's Athletes in WWII*; and coauthor of *Duty, Honor, Applause: America's Entertainers in WWII*. *George S. Patton: On Guts, Glory, and Winning* and *Mark Twain: His Words, Wit, and Wisdom* (cowritten with Michael Richards) are the first two books in a series on American Icons. He lives in south Kansas City, Missouri.